# Old Maine Woman

Stories from The Coast
to The County

*by Glenna Johnson Smith*

Also from Islandport Press


*Where Cool Waters Flow* by Randy Spencer

*Contentment Cove* and *Young* by Miriam Colwell

*Stealing History* by William D. Andrews

*Windswept*, *Mary Peters*, and *Silas Crockett* by Mary Ellen Chase

*My Life in the Maine Woods* by Annette Jackson

*Shoutin' into the Fog* by Thomas Hanna

*Nine Mile Bridge* by Helen Hamlin

*In Maine* by John N. Cole

*The Cows Are Out!* by Trudy Chambers Price

*Hauling by Hand* by Dean Lawrence Lunt

*down the road a piece: A Storyteller's Guide to Maine* by John McDonald

*Live Free and Eat Pie: A Storyteller's Guide to New Hampshire* by Rebecca Rule

*Not Too Awful Bad: A Storyteller's Guide to Vermont* by Leon Thompson

*A Moose and a Lobster Walk into a Bar* by John McDonald

*At One: In a Place Called Maine* by Lynn Plourde and Leslie Mansmann

*The Little Fisherman* by Margaret Wise Brown and Dahlov Ipcar

*The Cat at Night* by Dahlov Ipcar

*My Wonderful Christmas Tree* by Dahlov Ipcar


These and other Maine books are available at:
www.islandportpress.com

# Old Maine Woman

## Stories from The Coast to The County

*by Glenna Johnson Smith*

ISLANDPORT PRESS

ISLANDPORT PRESS • YARMOUTH

ISLANDPORT PRESS
P.O. Box 10
Yarmouth, Maine 04096
www.islandportpress.com
books@islandportpress.com

ISBN: 978-1-934031-41-4
Library of Congress Card Number: 2010937793

Book jacket design by Karen F. Hoots / Hoots Design
Book designed by Michelle A. Lunt / Islandport Press
Publisher Dean L. Lunt
Cover image of Glenna courtesy of Lorraine Wilcox
All other photos courtesy of Glenna Johnson Smith

*To my three sons Steven, Byron, and Melbourne Smith.*
*My boys—my heroes.*

# Acknowledgments

MY GRATITUDE to Kathryn Olmstead for publishing my pieces in *Echoes* magazine for more than twenty years. Her excellent editing has helped me to improve, and her encouragement has kept me writing. If she had not organized my essays and stories and submitted them to Islandport Press, this book would never have happened.

A thank-you to Mary-Ann McHugh, assistant editor at *Echoes*, for her honest appraisals and her friendship.

Thanks to Gordon Hammond, whose drawings enhanced many of my *Echoes* pieces.

I am grateful to Dean Lunt, Amy Canfield, and others at Islandport Press for putting up with my slowness and my indecision, and for making my impossible dream come true.

—

# Table of Contents

# Foreword

THE WRITING in these essays and short fiction
pieces is lyrical and steady, humorous and yet pensive, nostalgic
but always optimistic. That could be a description that perfectly
fits the author as well.

The word *elder* is used in many societies as a term of respect
for the older members of a group or clan. With the wisdom of
the years, they are the ones, after all, best prepared to counsel
younger members, to guide and educate them. This would also
be the best word to describe Glenna Smith except that, well,
she's so darn young. When I first met Glenna, she was a few
years past her seventieth birthday and driving about in a little
red sports car, windows down and wind in her hair. Once, she
drove me from Presque Isle to Fort Kent in that same car. As I
watched her drive, I remember thinking, "I hope there are little
red sports cars in heaven." Another time, we sat up into the very
late hours of a special night reciting the poetry we both loved.
She's an elder, all right, there's no doubt about that. But she's the
youngest elder I've ever known.

Glenna has touched so many young people by the example
she has set for them. She has taught us all how to face each day
with humor, courage, and the sure knowledge that life is the
greatest gift of all. In the essays that follow, we long for the
Model T that Glenna would like to keep in her backyard as a
pet. "In summer I'd fill the backseat with pots of geraniums," she
writes. By remembering her youth in these pages, she brings
back to life percale dresses that cost ninety-eight cents, the
importance of hanging on to a perfectly good button, rumble
seats, and an old-world politeness we could use more of today.
Glenna writes that she's not up to modern notions such as
computers, e-mail, and cell phones because she has "a 1920-model

brain." Well, that might be true, but let's consider that statement. It was in 1920 that the League of Women Voters was founded. It was the year of the first transatlantic two-way radio broadcast, an event that probably rivaled the cell phone in its day. Women's suffrage was guaranteed when the 19th Amendment to the Constitution was passed. Babe Ruth was sold to the New York Yankees and the "Curse of the Bambino" was loosed on the Red Sox. The first commercial radio station made its debut broadcast, a happening that would match the first satellite dish marching into town today. And out in Hollywood an actor named Douglas Fairbanks married the lovely Mary Pickford. This was the world Glenna Smith was born into, and this is the history she brings with her into the current millennium. Her memories begin with a childhood spent in Down East Maine, with a view of the ocean, instead of those open and windy potato fields of Aroostook County that she grew to love and claim as home.

She is more modern than she will ever realize, and the reason is that she is ageless. She is akin to lichen, which can adjust to any surface, any climate, any idea. I've lost count of the young people who have told me that Glenna Smith is their mentor, their role model, their champion. You cannot counsel the young unless you hear their voices and listen closely to their words. To do that, you don't need the old wall telephone that would be the first Glenna used as a child; nor do you need the latest cell phone, what she refers to as "a tiny spaceship with its eerie blue lights." You simply need the human heart, open to new ideas, patient and loving. Glenna has that in spades.

People often ask, "How did we live before cell phones and digital cameras and a million television stations?" In this book, and in how she lives her life as example, Glenna Smith, our young elder, shows us how.

Cathie Pelletier
Allagash, Maine
October 2010

# Introduction

I AM A PRODUCT of rural Maine—twenty-one years in Hancock County, the other sixty-nine in Aroostook. Although no two of us are alike, I've observed attitudes that seem typical of many country people, past and present.

Most of my relatives and neighbors in both counties have valued hard work. One of the greatest compliments given at funerals: "She/he was a hard worker." The last words spoken to me by my great-grandmother Addie Lassell, then in her nineties, were, "Every day work hard at something worthwhile, Glenna. That's the important thing." She didn't have to tell me that she enjoyed every day—I could see that.

Most country people take responsibility for their families. They treat their farm animals well, and neighbors look out for each other. Rural people may not talk about love and loyalty, but they know their value. Most of us try to do right, but when we mess up we can laugh at ourselves and start over. Because I am one of the rural everyday people, I like to write about us.

My life has been a long walk on wondrous paths. Many people have walked a piece with me along the way: grandparents, parents, neighbors, summer people, mentors, schoolmates, colleagues, students, sons, grandchildren, great-grandchildren, dear friends, and a few true loves. All have given me a bit of themselves. These bits are a part of who I am and what I write about.

# Part One

In my early years I felt snug and secure in Ashville, in Maine's Hancock County, where houses were close together and where low hills sheltered us from the howling winds of fierce storms. Always I liked looking out at Frenchman Bay with its islands and at Bar Harbor and Cadillac Mountain across the bay.

*Glenna with her mother, Kathleen Proctor Johnson*

*Glenna, about age two*

# Ashville Summers

"THERE ARE TIMES when the only vacation spot in the world is the past." I don't know who wrote that, but I think of it when I want to run away from the present. My trips to the past often take me to summers in the 1920s.

Back then in Ashville, there were no swimming lessons, Little League baseball programs, or arts and crafts classes. We ate breakfast at 5:30, Papa went off to work, and Mama said to me, "Go out and play now, dear." Since she had to run the post office, I was free. I don't think it crossed her mind that any harm could come to me, for she gave me no warnings or instructions.

When my appetite told me it was time for lunch—or dinner, as we called it—I wandered back to the house. I don't recall that other kids' mothers checked up on them, either. For one thing, all the adults had to work hard at necessary chores. Beyond that, they must have felt that all the wide spaces around the village were safe playgrounds.

I remember the joy of early morning—birds singing, dew shining on the grass, a cool breeze blowing off the bay, the new sun throwing shadows on the land. I ran off in one direction or another with little planning. I might meet up with other kids and we might play together for a while, or not. We seemed to run in and out of each other's summer days. Sometimes I would run through a field that in one corner smelled of sweetgrass. I knew the old Indian in town picked the sweetgrass for making baskets. I'd run faster if a little green snake or toad startled me. I'd run very fast by Aunt Tune's little house, for I thought she was a witch, and she'd kill me and eat me if she got the chance. I could never understand why Mama was so nice to her, always providing her with meals. Next I might run to the shore and climb to the top of my rock. I would hide in a niche at the top and sail away for adventures on the high seas. If the tide came in and surrounded my rock I had to wade up to my knees to get ashore. At low tide I'd scrunch down so the clam diggers wouldn't see me. I'd listen to them, and they'd become either the pirates who captured me or the heroes who saved me.

Sometimes I'd walk up to Corris's house and we'd play on a nearby ledge, our castle. While I was up there I might sail stick boats in the millstream. Later I would climb the rocky hill to the forest where Papa and other men cut their firewood. I loved the smell of the woodpiles. Up there I could pick and eat mint berries and chew the leaves. I knew places and times for wild

*Glenna, left, and her childhood friend Corris Martin, with their dolls*

4

strawberries, blueberries, blackberries, and raspberries. Sometimes I would fill a tin peanut-butter pail with berries for Mama. Sometimes I'd pick buttercups and daisies for her.

I ate clover blossoms and played with baby grasshoppers that lived in the spit on the daisy plants. Sometimes I tasted the milk of the milkweed plants. It was bitter, but my stick people, those I made and housed in the hollowed-out center of a thick clump of alder bushes, drank it regularly.

I liked to climb, too. When I climbed the pine tree on the ridge I could see the bay and the islands. The tree was the mast of my tall ship. Often I climbed the cemetery fence behind the church. From there I could reach the wide lower branches of the ash tree. I could daydream there, looking up at the sky through the leafy branches. Sometimes I'd fall asleep. One day, old Emma Carpenter came to the cemetery and pulled weeds around little markers of the graves of her children. I kept very still so she wouldn't see me. I felt sad to see her there, for I knew none of her babies lived to grow up. I asked Mama why Emma didn't cry when she went to the graves. She said, "Emma never lets on."

I loved it when the older girls, Edna and Leola, played with us little kids. Sometimes we played Green Light and Giant Step. Sometimes I played with Edna's brother, Elliot, who was my age. We spent many hours in the gravel pit, making roads and towns for rock families. Often we fought.

Once a farmer let us kids ride from the field to the barn on a hay load. We were a mile in the air, the hayrack creaked, and the hay was prickly, but it smelled wonderful. I also liked to sit quietly beside a big pine-tree root, for I knew in the space under it there were little people. I knew that if I were patient, someday they would come out. I did see them, but only in my dreams.

Back then we all had jackknives for whittling whistles and boats, digging spruce gum off the trees, and playing mumbletypeg. We would put the sharp blade on our knee, forehead, or nose and

snap it into the ground. I don't remember that we ever cut ourselves or each other.

I wasn't allowed to have a bicycle because my father thought
they weren't safe, but Elliott let me ride his. One day it got away
from me. I went fast down a hill and crashed on a rock pile.
Elliott ran home and told my mother.

"Where's Glenna?" she asked.

"Dead, I guess, on the rock pile," he said. "But my wheel is
bent. You've got to buy me a new one."

I was bruised, and punished for riding a bike. Papa repaired
the wheel.

Our parents were justified most of the time in allowing us to
run free. Or maybe we were just lucky. We didn't drown in the
bay or the mill pond, we weren't harmed by wild animals, we
weren't poisoned by any plants, and we didn't fall out of trees
and break our necks.

In those summers, I knew that the whole world belonged to
me. Never since the 1920s have I been so rich or so free.

# String Too Short to Save

TODAY I WATCHED a man throw my week's accumulation of garbage into the maw of a giant truck. I don't consider myself wasteful, but as the noisy machine chewed my trash I could imagine my mother's scowl of disapproval.

I can't recall from my childhood in the 1920s that we had any garbage to speak of. In many ways my mother was like all the other women, but she did have a reputation for being more frugal than most, because she had been brought up by a grandmother who was considered a miserly recluse. Like Grammie Knight, Mama never did join in the American excitement of throwing away the old and buying new from the Five and Dime Store.

As a conforming teenager I was sometimes embarrassed that Mama didn't buy ninety-eight-cent flowered percale house-dresses like other women wore. Summer people gave her boxes of clothes. She ran the post office, but she kept her sewing machine in a window where she could see approaching customers, and at odd moments she would darn, patch, and make items over for herself, me, relatives, and neighbor kids.

Although I often thought she looked bizarre, she enjoyed her secondhand finery. For many winters she wore a maroon wool dress that went through a variety of collars and cuffs. My favorite was a lovely beige lace set cut from the discarded underpants of a summer lady.

Once Mama made me a dark-green wool skirt. "What will I say," I complained, "if people ask me if this was something of my grandmother's that you made over?"

She gave me her sweet-smug smile. "This cloth comes from a suit your Great-Grandmother Lassell had made, back in the 1890s." I must admit I liked that skirt and wore it through high school and college. When I outgrew it, Mama took it back, and I suspect that somewhere in a wool quilt or braided rug, pieces of that green serge still live.

Mama patched and darned sheets and tablecloths, and when they finally had to be discarded she cut them into pieces, ironed them, and packed them neatly for emergencies. Once a young family was burned out, and Mama's old, soft white pieces served for diapers, crib sheets, and handkerchiefs. Often they were used for bandages.

When a much-patched dress was too worn to wear, Mama saved the buttons, snaps, buckles, and hooks and eyes. Then for future quilts she cut up any pieces that still held together. In later years she never could understand why people bought new cloth for quilt making. The whole point of quilting was to get something beautiful and warm from discards.

Remember this old joke?

"What's in this box, Emma?"

"String too short to save."

That could have been written about Mama. She saved every greeting card that came to our house, cut out the pictures, stuck them into scrapbooks, and sent them once a year to be given to people in a hospital's contagious diseases ward. Since she was using something a second time it didn't bother her that a scrapbook had to be burned when the patient could no longer look at it.

Mama loved making doll clothes from scraps and never forgave me for having all sons. What fun she would have had with her great-granddaughters, my dear granddaughters!

Mama was a talented cook, but saved food just as much as she saved everything else. Although we had neither icebox nor refrigerator (only the rich had them), none of our food ever spoiled. She went every day to the butcher or else the fish man came by, and she bought just enough for the day. What was left from noon appeared at supper in a salad, stew, or casserole. If there happened to be an extra serving, Mama would take it across the hill to old Aunt Tune. Although there were no surplus food programs, I suspect it was a rare day when Aunt Tune, who lived alone, didn't receive a bowl of stew, some johnnycake, and a piece of pie from someone.

But back to the garbage. I tell myself that something must have been thrown out back then. Not shoes—Papa learned to put on new soles and heels. Not old pots and pans with holes in them—they could be patched. Not old magazines—they were given to shut-ins. Wastepaper was needed to build the three wood fires. The kitchen stove was lit every day for cooking and heating the water tank, but my parents didn't believe in heating a room with nobody in it, so the post office stove wasn't lit on Sundays, and the living room stove was lit only on Sundays and an occasional evening. We slept in cold bedrooms, but that was no punishment. My bed had a feather tick and blanket sheets, and on cold nights, smooth hot rocks from the oven, wrapped in old pieces of blanket. The rocks cooled off in the night, but by that time I was so cozy and warm that it didn't matter. I still like to sleep in a cold room.

Because Mama raised and canned her own vegetables and picked and preserved her own fruit and berries, we had few tin cans to discard. Lard and peanut butter came in little pails, which were used forever after for berry picking. She took a cloth bag to the grocery store, much like today's shoppers are urged to do, and her own dish to the butcher and the fish man, so there were no disposable wrappings.

The few table scraps—peelings and all—went to a neighbor's pig, or were thrown in a little pit behind the house. What the small animals and birds didn't eat became compost. Out of that pile grew the biggest blackberries in town.

One of Mama's recyclings bothered a few squeamish neighbors. We had no indoor plumbing, and our outhouse was behind the little barn where Papa kept the Model T. Behind the outhouse was the reddest, healthiest stand of rhubarb anywhere around. "Why waste a good source of fertilizer?" Mama would ask. Some hardy souls came to pick it, and even the ones who didn't would not refuse a second piece of Mama's creamy rhubarb pie topped with high peaks of meringue.

Although we had few of the world's goods in the 1920s, I can't say that I felt deprived. Once when I was very young I asked Papa if we were rich or poor. He thought before he answered, "Poor, I guess." I would have believed "rich." I had good food to eat, clean clothes, a safe and quiet world for dreaming and playing, and a comfortable bed for sleep. What else could "rich" provide?

As she grew older Mama was aghast at American throwaway consumption. "It has to stop," she'd say. "There isn't enough for everyone forever." But many of us of my generation in our modern wisdom looked around at the woods and empty spaces. We pointed with pride at our technology and our spewing smokestacks and said of course there'll always be enough.

If Kathleen Proctor Johnson were around today she'd be proud of her grandsons and their wives, who use their resources carefully and respect the environment. Yet, if she could see what a garbage dump many of us are making of our world, I think we'd see her pursed lips and scowly smile and she'd say, "Why didn't you listen?"

# Ashville Sunday School Picnic

EVEN THOUGH it was called the Sunday School Picnic, every child in the village and out on the side roads was invited, Sunday School member or not. Their mothers and grandmothers and any aunts who happened to be around were invited, too. Our hosts were Mr. and Mrs. William J. Schieffelin, summer residents from New York City, Park Avenue to be exact, who owned a peninsula that jutted into Frenchman Bay. Every year the picnic was held at their Dutch colonial mansion, which they called "the cottage," and which we natives called "the big house" to distinguish it from the peninsula's smaller summer homes that belonged to several Schieffelin sons and daughters.

The house was a magic place to us village children, with its wide, pillared porches on the front and one side, acres of lawns, gardens, and trees, a swimming pool and tennis court, a view of the bay, and the family yacht and sailboats.

Waiting for picnic day was like waiting for Christmas. We counted down days and then hours. We agonized over the possibility that rain would fall on picnic day. I don't recall that it ever did.

When the day arrived we all met at the post office, where I lived. If we were to be picked up at ten o'clock, many of us were scrubbed, dressed in our best, and waiting by eight, with stern warnings from mothers to keep clean until the cars came.

Although the ride to the estate took only a few minutes, it was a big part of the excitement. Captain Albee, the estate overseer, would drive up in the woody station wagon; his son Emery, the chauffeur, would drive the long, pea-green touring car, which I think was a Lincoln but might have been a Cadillac. Between the front and back seats of the touring car were footrests, which converted into buddy seats for children. They were the ride of choice. Since each vehicle made several trips, some boys would keep waiting until they could get a buddy seat.

When we arrived at the back lawn, our hosts were there to greet us. Mr. Schieffelin, a tall, apple-cheeked Dutchman clad in tweed knickers and a cashmere sweater, and Mrs. Schieffelin, tall and beautiful in a pastel skirt and silk blouse, led us to the front porch. There the local women, ensconced in white wicker chairs and settees with flowered chintz covers, spent the most leisurely day of their summer. Mrs. Schieffelin, her daughters, and daughters-in-law visited with them throughout the day as the local women watched their children running races on the lawn and gazed out at the bay and the islands. Many of them had worked on the estate during the summers of their youth; many still did spring cleaning or laundry or cooking for some of the households. But on this one day, they were waited upon by Maude, the maid from England, and Janet, from Scotland. The maids, clad in their daytime uniforms of blue striped cotton with white aprons and caps, served cut-glass cups of punch all day, and a delicious meal at noon. I marvel that we children were allowed to drink from the cut-glass cups, too. People of lesser class would have given us paper cups.

I was in awe of Mrs. Schieffelin. When I was old enough to work at the big house, about thirteen or fourteen, I admired a picture of her as the most outstanding debutante the year of her coming out. I had never seen anyone so beautiful. Her hair was silver white, and, piled up on her head, it looked soft as a cloud. She was tall, slender, and stately. I felt sorry for all the queens of Europe because, grand as they were, none was as queenly as Louise Schieffelin. Yet she would chat with us village folk, showing us the same kindness and respect accorded to her friends and family.

On the wide lawn, which sloped down to the bay, we children, led by the Schieffelin children and older grandchildren, entered contests. There were egg-in-spoon races, three-legged races, blindfold races, and sack races. I wasn't expert at any of them, but I gave my worst performance at eating crackers and peanut butter and then whistling "The Star-Spangled Banner." Even under ideal conditions, I couldn't whistle "The Star-Spangled Banner."

Somehow at the end of the day each of us got at least one prize, even if it were third prize in a race involving three contestants. I believe that Etta Hammond, the Sunday School superintendent, gathered information about each of us, and Mrs. Schieffelin chose the prizes. Anyway, we always seemed to get exactly what we wanted, be it a book, a doll, a truck, a paint set, or a game. Each of the women received a gift, too. Often it was a lovely little vase with flowers from the picking garden, arranged by Maude, who, although she claimed she hated every minute of it, did wonderful things with flowers.

The luncheon menu never varied, and how disappointed we would have been if it had. There was creamed chicken, green peas, rice, hot rolls, a summer salad, ice cream, and cake. The two big crystal punch bowls were filled many times, one with raspberry punch, the other with lime. Chunks of ice and sprigs of mint floated in the bowls.

During the day, Captain Albee gave the women yacht rides around the islands or across the bay to Bar Harbor. In the afternoon we children were allowed to go to the playground, where there were swings, slides, and a merry-go-round, which was spun around by hand, and a big sandbox with toys.

We never wanted to go home; however, the ride home might be a chance to sit in a buddy seat. We looked back on the picnic for as long as we had looked forward to it. Although I usually felt inferior at school contests, I didn't mind not winning races at the picnic. I always felt I was a person of value there.

In addition to providing the picnic, Mrs. Schieffelin had a big hand in our Christmases. She sent spectacular decorations for the church tree, and a gift for every child in the village, usually a more wonderful present than any of our parents could afford. Years later I asked maids Janet and Maude if they had to go to Macy's and pick out the presents. They said they went along to help, but that Madame, her list in hand, picked out every single one. I can still remember my favorite from the Schieffelins—a delicately crafted Noah's Ark with beautifully sculpted and painted animals. I played with them for years in a sandbox my father built.

There are few of us left who remember the buddy seats, the red and green punch, the three-legged races, and the creamed chicken. There are few left who knew the graciousness and the goodness of Mrs. Louise Schieffelin, who gave us childhood memories that enriched our entire lives.

# Pettee's Cash Store

I WAS BROUGHT UP in Pettee's Cash Store. Although the faded sign read W. M. PETTEE, PROPRIETOR, by 1921, when my parents moved in with their baby, the store had been abandoned. Mr. Pettee was long gone, having left all his dry goods and patent medicines on the shelves and in the drawers. Because adults did not discuss in the presence of little ears such delicate matters as money, illness, and death, I never knew the fate of Mr. Pettee. Although Mama often pointed out that we were only renters, I never knew who owned the big old building.

"Why don't you whitewash this place?" a neighbor would ask. "Why don't you throw away the stuff in the drawers? Nothing there's worth a plugged nickel."

"We don't own it," Mama would answer. "It's not ours to tamper with."

And tamper she didn't. She wouldn't throw out a bottle of Lydia Pinkham's Compound for Female Complaints, a package of liver pills, or a tin of chewing tobacco. With equal zeal she guarded the contents of the deep drawers in the long counters— feather hats, high-buttoned boots, lacy shawls, high-necked blouses with leg o'mutton sleeves.

Sometimes a teacher or a Grange member would ask if she could borrow some of the clothes for a play. "As far's I'm concerned you can," Mama would answer, "but they're not mine to lend." It was as if she expected W. M. Pettee to reconstruct himself someday right there in the middle of the store and demand a tally of every darning needle, crochet hook, and shingle nail.

*This is the Ashville Post Office, where Glenna grew up. The family's bedrooms were upstairs. On the step of the Post Office is Glenna's Aunt Annie Thompson, who came to stay with Glenna and her mother during the winter, probably 1925, when Glenna's father was living in Danvers, Mass., to learn cabinetry and carpentry from his Uncle Jesse.*

Mama spent most of her time in a tiny cubicle at the front corner of the store, where she presided as postmistress. Outside her niche the changes were few. Mama had added racks for displaying the newspapers, magazines, and cards she sold, and along the back wall behind the old yellow velvet couch where the dog slept there were perhaps a hundred books, a lending library supplied and often replenished by our Sunday School picnic providers, the Schieffelin family. In the front near the windows was the treadle sewing machine, where Mama would mend for us or sew for the "heathen" Chinese who were prayed for by the church missionary society. In the middle of the room beside Mr. Pettee's iron stove and woodbox was Papa's chair where he rocked and read library books when he wasn't away doing carpentry work. Mama's Martha Washington geraniums thrived in all the windows. "Kathleen has a green thumb," everybody said. Actually she used a lot of cow manure. Other than these few changes, Mr. Pettee would have found everything as he left it.

Today's human service organizations might declare Pettee's store an unfit place for a child. For one thing, it was always cold in the winter. Mama was terrified of burning the place down—perhaps because it wasn't hers to burn—so when Papa was away she would use barely enough wood to take the chill off. She bundled herself and me in long underwear and heavy wool skirts and sweaters, and the customers came dressed for outdoors anyway, so nobody suffered. It was drafty, though, as I played on the floor with its wide, splintery, unpainted boards, and its cracks big enough to swallow up needles, pennies, buttons, pencil stubs, and puzzle pieces. Since there was no cellar under the store, these treasures were lost forever. Yet even though the dingy, cobwebbed place with its dim kerosene lights and lack of plumbing would be a slum dwelling by today's standards, I loved all that space and freedom.

I was free because Mama was so busy she'd forget about me. Between customers she had to run back to the shed-like kitchen and keep the cookstove going, for there was always something baking or stewing for the next meal. On Monday she pumped and heated water and carried it to the washtubs in the back shed. There she scrubbed and rinsed, and lugged white goods back to the stove for boiling. Then she traveled back and forth to the clothesline. On Tuesday she spent hours at the ironing board. Throughout each day Mama took mini-vacations, dashing upstairs to make beds and empty slop pails and hurrying to the garden to pick a squash for a pie, all the while running back to the office every time the bell tinkled. Only in the afternoon did she lock the door and make a quick trip to the store. Although Mama cooked meals in a few minutes here and there, we never had a breakfast without hot biscuits and oatmeal, never a supper without hot biscuits and a pie, along with fish, potatoes, vegetables, and home-canned fruits, berries, and pickles.

It's no wonder that Mama could forget she had a daughter. Sometimes if she hadn't seen me for a few hours she'd scowl and say, "Where have you been, young lady?" I'd smile and say, "Just out to play, Mama." Satisfied, she'd ask no more questions.

Indoors on rainy days there were lovely spaces, too. The spooky shed chamber was filled with crates and boxes that I could push around to make castles, or I could curl up with the dog on the old yellow couch and look at the fairy tale pictures and gold-decorated oriental prints in the library books. And what Mama didn't know for a long time was that often I hid in the store on wide, dark shelves behind counters, or even in the greasy, gray mailbags under the post office table. I would keep still for a long time, hoping I'd hear stuff not meant for children's ears. A woman would say to Mama, "Kathleen, where's your ya'one?" And Mama would say, "Out to play." Then there'd be a tale about what Elise went through having her baby, and land sakes, her married only three months. And there were the horrors and the dangers of the marriage bed. One woman said, "All Rupert has to do is throw his pants on the bedpost and I'm that way again." I had no idea what "that way" was, but my imagination ran wild. I liked the stories about which husbands were running where with that awful woman up the Pond Road, the one who painted her face and put henna in her hair. I never knew Mama to peddle any gossip she heard, but she was a good listener. And so was I!

But one day I stretched my luck too far. It's a wonder Mama didn't lock the mailbag and send me off to Siam. Hiram Kingsley was outside the little window where mail was dispensed, talking to Mama in her office. Hiram was an ancient and cranky bachelor who had lived all his life on the home farm with his sister Patience, a spinster. I feared Hiram, but I was fascinated by his false teeth. They didn't fit and stayed clamped together when he talked. I heard that he took them out when he ate, but he wore them for dress-up when he came to the village. I loved the funny way the teeth made him talk, and on that fateful day I just had to see what I sounded like when I talked with my teeth clamped together. Unfortunately I was in a mailbag not a yard from Mama's feet.

"Good morning, Kathleen," Hiram said.

"Good morning, Kathleen," I said.

"Is that your pesky ya'one talking?" Hiram asked.

"Is that your pesky ya'one talking?" I asked.

The sharp toe of Mama's size-three shoe was kicking mailbags and coming closer and closer to my sanctuary.

"That ya'one's hide needs a good tanning," Hiram said.

"You're right," Mama said, hauling me from cover and pushing me down in the chair by the stove.

"You going to whip her?" Hiram asked.

"No," Mama said, "I'll leave that for her father to tend to."

How I dreaded those delayed spankings with Papa's leather slipper. And how he must have hated coming home from work eager to get back to reading his book only to find he had to paddle his kid when he wasn't even mad.

Hiram glared at me, and I smiled at him.

"I may send her up to bed," Mama said.

Although my bed was warm and cozy at night, I didn't want to go up there during the cold day. I racked my brain for something to say so Hiram would forget about immediate punishment. Finally it came to me. "Do you sleep with Patience on cold nights?" I asked.

19

I couldn't understand why he stormed out, slammed the door, dashed for his horse and sleigh, and tore off up the road. I wondered why Mama was so mad. I guess Papa was mad, too, when Mama told him, but I thought he almost wanted to laugh.

Anyway, the spanking was a stinging one, and since Mama was on to me, I had to be extra careful where I hid after that. Still, with all its hazards, it was fun living in Pettee's store.

# Dear Old Friend

THANK YOU for the letter that I found nestled in my P.O. box under frantic orders to SAVE! ATTEND ONCE-IN-A-LIFETIME SALE! VOTE FOR ME AND I'LL SAVE MAINE! SUBSCRIBE AND BECOME BEAUTIFUL, RICH, AND WISE!

As I was removing the contents of my box I noticed others doing the same. Then we formed a little procession to the waste can and deposited our junk mail. I was lucky—I had your letter to take home. Some of my fellow travelers went away empty-handed, but left the waste can almost full. What a waste of trees.

I felt like a real person as I poured coffee and settled into my favorite chair. I could see your smile and hear your voice as I read your words. A letter addressed to me only, written by someone who knows my smile and my voice—a letter from a friend is a wonderful thing.

In my earliest memories, the arrival of the mail carrier was the high point of my day. Because my mother was postmistress, I got to watch the whole process every day: the neighbors gathering fifteen minutes early, standing and talking outdoors in good weather, hugging the big iron stove on bad days. Old Peter Addison would say, "Mail's late today," and Mama would give him her vague smile and say, "Not due for another ten minutes, Peter."

Finally, we'd hear the clatter of the Model T truck. Everybody watched as it wheezed to a halt, and as Adam Haskell dragged the greasy, gray bags from the truck body. He'd come through the door complaining.

"Not enough mail today for me to bother getting out of bed!" Or, "More catalogs! Montgomery Ward and Sears Roebuck were plenty, but now—National Bellas Hess! Every one of 'em bigger 'n the Bible. They want me to break my back? First thing you know people will be ordering more stuff they don't need. Then I'll have to drag in all those packages."

In her closed-in cubicle, Mama would empty each bag on the counter and place the contents into the boxes. The impatient could watch through the little glass door with their number on it.

"Oh, there's a letter from my sister! Hand it out now, will you, Kathleen?"

The curious would watch all the boxes. Annie Lawson would say, "Land, there's a big, purple envelope in Perkins's box. Did you notice who it was from, Kathleen?"

Mama annoyed her by putting the letters in the boxes face-down and by giving her the absentminded smile that said, "I didn't hear your question."

When Ellen Handy was so in love with Paul Eaton that she couldn't see straight, he took a job in a shoe factory in Gardiner. Every day Ellen sent him a fat letter with SWAK written on the outside. (I asked Mama what SWAK meant; she told me not to be a nosy child.) For a few weeks Paul answered, and then his letters tapered off. Ellen would watch her box, and then say, "Kathleen, are you sure there isn't a letter stuck in the bottom of the mailbag? Will you just check again, please?" She'd be fighting tears when she left for home. "I hope I never fall in love," I'd say to myself.

When Jane Dyer got a rare and short note from her son in New Jersey, she'd tear it open and read it aloud. " 'Dear Mama, We're all well and hope you are the same. The weather's been hot this summer. The kids are growing fast. Love, Bill.' My, doesn't he write a good letter!"

Second only to the letters was the excitement generated by the arrival of the magazines Mama sold. Women waited eagerly for the next installment of the continued stories in *The Delineator*, *Woman's Home Companion*, and *Ladies' Home Journal*.

"Kathleen, are you sure my magazine isn't back there on a shelf somewhere? It's a week late, and that poor soul was in such a predicament at the end of last month's chapter . . . "

"It's not due until next Tuesday," Mama would say.

Women waited desperately for *True Story* and *True Love*. Men yearned for *Wild West* and *True Adventure*. Whole families read the weeklies, *Liberty* and *Saturday Evening Post*. Some children took *Boys' Life*. (Was there a magazine for girls? I can't remember.) Because money was scarce in the 1920s and '30s, magazines got swapped around the neighborhood, amid complaints when somebody spilled coffee on somebody else's *Silver Screen*.

As soon as I could read and write, I wanted to get mail of my own. My first letters came from my father, who worked in Danvers, Massachusetts, the winter I was five. A few years later, Mama would give me stamped envelopes—I think they were two cents each—and I would cut coupons from the discarded magazines and send for free samples.

I got travel brochures from Australia and from the Grand Canyon, and information about schools, camps, and colleges—the kinds rich people attended. But best of all, I got samples of makeup and perfume. I had to scrub off the Tangee lipstick and the Evening in Paris perfume before Papa caught me, though.

I was excited and frightened by chain letters, which usually asked for money. "Send a dollar to each of the next five names on the list, and in a few weeks you'll receive a fortune! Add five new names to the list. Break the chain and bad luck will befall you." Some letters asked for Bible verses or recipes instead of money, but the results were just as serious. And there were examples of the bad luck—the man near Portland who broke the chain and then his barn burned. A Fort Kent woman broke the chain, and her son fell out of a tree and broke his leg.

Mama quoted post office law and said all chain letters that came to our house had to be thrown in the wastebasket. With each discard I waited in terror for the lightning to strike, the tidal wave to rush in.

Then there were the pen pal letters, names and addresses supplied by school publications. Years later, when I was teaching at Easton Grammar School, I joined my students in writing to a pen pal in Brazil. The kids enjoyed this project, but the answer I received from a young woman read something like this: "I will write to you only this one time, so don't answer. I wish to correspond only with the American man. But I will tell you some things about my country. We have this wonderful hot, brown drink called coffee. I wish you could taste it, but I know the plant doesn't grow in the North . . . "

But back to my post office days. My most troublesome mail came from companies that sent their goods unsolicited, and then demanded payment or the return of their product later. Once I received a little packet of worthless stamps, which my parents instructed me to throw away.

"This practice is illegal," Mama said. So for the next several years I received letters that said the company wanted a dollar or their stamps. At first they were polite: "We feel you have forgotten to pay . . . " But they grew progressively frightening: "Do you want your neighbors to know you can't be trusted?" And a few weeks later: "We are putting this matter in the hands of a collection agency." And in another few weeks, "One of our agents will come to your home to collect this money."

I begged Mama to send the dollar and spare my life, but she held out. Every time a stranger came through the post office door I'd whisper to Mama, "Is it the stamp man?"

"Don't be silly," she'd say. "They won't send someone all the way from New York just for a dollar." But I wasn't so sure.

Finally I began to get mail of my own from kids I met at 4-H Club state conventions. One girl wrote funny-looking letters with all the words around in a circle. A boy wrote puns: "I pine fir yew. Spruce up and write to me, Oak-A? Cedar address on the envelope."

I grew old enough to cry over the lyrics of a cowboy song: "Write me a letter, send it by mail, send it in care of Birmingham Jail . . ." And inevitably, I fell in love, wrote fat, daily letters with SWAK on the outside, and died a little when the object of my love stopped answering them.

But for all of my days, I have treasured letters from relatives and friends. Sometimes I forget to answer them, but I treasure them all the same. An envelope with my name in somebody's handwriting, a piece of paper inside with words written to me . . .

I like this quote from A. R. Gurney's play, *Love Letters*: "This is just me, the way I write . . . the way I want to be to you, giving myself to you across a distance . . . giving this piece of myself to you totally, and you can tear me up and throw me out, or keep me and read me today, tomorrow, anytime until you die."

Love,
Glenna

25

# I Hated Sunday

WHEN I WAS A KID I hated Sunday even
though the day started out good. For breakfast Mama made flap-
jacks in the iron spider, I liked the scary Old Testament stories
in Sunday School, and even church got exciting at times when
the Methodist preacher raised his voice until it echoed off the
tin ceiling as he warned us where we'd go if we persisted in
drinking, smoking, dancing, card playing, swearing, and reading
modern novels. Through it all, his great fist pointed down,
down, down. For years I thought Hell was in the church basement. Then Sunday afternoon dinner was delicious chicken and
fixings, most of which Mama prepared on Saturday so she
wouldn't defile the Sabbath. But right after the dinner dishes
were done the day went to pieces.

We went to Grampie and Grammie Johnson's because Uncle
Henry had built them a radio from a kit. Papa always parked the
flivver under the living room window, hooked the radio to the
car battery, and tried to get station KDKA. I think they got
more squeals and static than anything else, but every week they
tried. Uncle Henry had provided four sets of earphones, and
since I had two parents and two grandparents, I didn't hear a
thing on Sunday afternoon.

I couldn't go out and play because that would break the
Sabbath. The only book I could look at was the Bible, which
Mama would put in my hands when she sat me on the couch. If
I walked I made static, and four pairs of eyes glared at me like
creatures from another world with enormous metal, wire-sprout-
ing ears. So I watched them bob their heads and tap their toes,

27

and assumed they were listening to a peppy hymn. Or I would see them give each other sage nods, and decide that the evangelist, Billy Sunday, had uttered a great truth.

Usually I opened the Bible to the color picture entitled "Moses in the Bulrushes" and stared at the baby tied with a pink bow to his little basket and floating along, tended by his dark-eyed sister who was wearing a filmy, low-necked thing not at all appropriate for wading in a swamp. Sometimes I'd make up wild adventures for the two of them. Good thing Mama and Papa didn't know I was doing that on Sunday.

At last, Billy Sunday's sermon ended, and then great-aunts and great-uncles dropped by. The men would say, "Let's have a look at her." The top would come off the radio, and they'd examine the rows of tubes the size of lightbulbs, and the tangle of colored wires. The great-aunts stood back, scowled, shook their heads, and asked, "Land, what won't they think of next?" Through all this I had to be seen and not heard.

Then came the lowest point of the day, when Grammie went to the kitchen to cook supper. After the big Sunday dinner earlier that day they felt they had to deny the flesh, so we always had cornmeal mush Sunday night—great lumpy mounds of yellow, gritty, tasteless mush. One day I asked why we couldn't have oatmeal, and I was told to be grateful to God for the food he provided. I never could bring myself to blame God for that mush. Then they assured me that far away there were millions of heathen Chinese who would love the meal. I doubted that. Why would they eat mush if they could have rice? And finally they pointed out that oatmeal was breakfast food. So I choked down my mush, Sunday after Sunday.

When we went home, Mama put me to bed with the reminder that I say my prayers and thank God for my blessings. So I thanked God that there wouldn't be another Sunday for six whole days.

# The Hawkins House

WHEN I PICTURE the big gray house near the
bay I see first the birds' nests with real eggs in them, still snug in
their real branches, hanging on the walls of the parlor. The blue
eggs in one nest looked as new and bright as if the robin mother
had just flown away for a minute, and yet the nests had hung
there for more than sixty years, collected by Mr. Hawkins who
moved up from Marblehead, Massachusetts, and built and fur-
nished the house. Although I knew the shells were brittle and
empty, I kept daydreaming that the little birds would peck their
way out, and fly through an open door and on to the pasture.

In my childhood I visited the Hawkins house every Tuesday
night to take a piano lesson from Miss Louise. My parents paid
her fifty cents an hour and had high hopes that she'd make me
into a musician. I can't remember how to play an arpeggio, but
I've never forgotten Miss Louise and her sister.

Although they were so different, Louise and Josephine
Hawkins always seemed to enjoy each other and the house.
Louise was a tiny, birdlike woman, straight and slender with shining gray hair piled high on her head. She wore long dark dresses
with lace collars and cuffs, and always around her neck was a
black velvet ribbon fastened with a white cameo pin. Once I
heard her explain why, with her musical little laugh: "Because it
hides my scrawny neck." Miss Josephine often said, "Louise is in
delicate health," and insisted that she rest often.

Josephine, taller and more robust, wore flowered house
dresses and aprons, did the cooking and cleaning, planted and
tended the garden, and taught the cats to sit up on little stools

and do tricks. She often mentioned that she loved keeping the house "just the way Mother and Father had it."

The house was the grandest I'd seen except for summer people's mansions. At the head of the polished staircase there was a real bathroom with a brass tub. All the gleaming furniture, wall paneling, and floors looked new; I couldn't imagine how children could have grown up there without wear and tear on the place.

I often stared at the pictures of handsome, manly boys and two lovely girls with shining eyes and dark curling hair. Once I asked my mother why those beautiful girls didn't marry, and she told me the town lore: Miss Josephine had been engaged to a man who was killed in the Spanish-American War, and she refused to give her heart to another. Miss Louise had been betrothed also, and her beloved had left her for another woman. She also refused to love again, and for her lifetime did kind deeds for the man who had jilted her, his wife, and their children. I have no idea whether those tales are true, for I never heard the Hawkins sisters mention their loves. But the stories made me sad; I wondered how those dear, elderly women could seem so jolly.

Often my mother visited with Miss Josephine during my music lesson, and then the four of us would have tea from delicate china cups, and cookies from cut-glass plates. (My tea was of the cambric variety, mostly hot milk.) Then we would visit until my father returned from a Lodge meeting and picked us up. I loved those evenings. I'd stare at the glowing fire and the brass andirons, and sometimes I was even allowed to work the ancient bellows to make the fire burn brighter. And I'd listen to every word of the wonderful stories the Hawkins sisters told. My favorite was about the day the girls, dressed in their high boots, long dresses, and petticoats, went out to play in the yard. They noticed two pairs of their brothers' trousers blowing on the clothesline, and when they realized nobody was in sight, they donned the pants and ran barefoot to the pasture.

"We were free!" Josephine said. "We ran and ran through the tall grass, and then we threw ourselves on the ground and rolled down the hill. We climbed the fence and we climbed the old pine tree. We were as happy as little puppies—or little boys."

"But then Father came out and caught us," Louise said. "We were punished and told that we must never wear men's clothing again. And of course we never did."

"And Mother said we'd placed a blot on the family honor," Josephine said, laughing. We all laughed, but I felt like crying.

Sometimes they'd seem to forget I was listening and would tell stories meant only for my mother's ears. Perhaps it was because they always gave me the comics section from the Boston paper. Yet although I read and reread *Billy the Boy Artist*, *The Katzenjammer Kids*, *Jiggs and Maggie*, and *Tillie the Toiler*, I didn't miss a word of their stories. The one that shocked and surprised me most was about a man who prowled around at night and frightened women who lived alone.

"When Louise and I were reading fairly late one night there was a loud knock on the front door," Josephine said. "We'd already locked up for the night, but I pulled the curtain aside, and we both peeked out. And there he was! He opened his coat and with the aid of his flashlight he exposed himself to us."

I thought how frightened and shocked they must have been, two poor helpless old women living alone. But Louise spoke: "I said, 'Why Josephine, look at that! See what we've been missing all these years!' " And they both broke into peals of laughter at the memory.

"When he saw us laughing he covered himself and ran away," Josephine said.

I will never forget going to the Hawkins house—walking up the long path to the front door, past the lilac bushes and the peonies. On a rainy May night their scent would get inside me and make me yearn for something, I didn't know what.

I will never forget the Hawkins sisters—two women, two girls—who seemed to live in harmony with the big gray house without ever pecking their way out of their shells.

# The Sears and Roebuck Wife

ACTUALLY, ORRIN Coombs got his wife from an advertisement in a magazine. Even though you could buy a buggy and a harness for the horse, even though you could order tires for the Model T, even though you could send for tombstones, the Sears and Roebuck catalog didn't offer wives.

Yet the neighbors continued to refer to her as the wife Orrin got from Sears and Roebuck. The truth is, for Orrin Coombs to get a wife by any means was beyond belief. He'd been a bachelor forever; he didn't even talk to people. Some said he was deaf, but others said he just didn't want to be bothered.

By hiding in the post office and listening to adult conversations I learned that he'd been in love with a girl once, but that she met up with a traveling man from Bangor and off she went. There were rumors that she died young and in terrible circumstances. Anyway, Orrin never looked at another woman. He just grew thinner and more stooped and got a thicker crust of smoke and grime from his blacksmith shop. When I was a kid I thought he was very old, but reckoning back, I guess he was in his early forties during the village-shattering year of the mail-order bride.

Orrin had found the name and address of a woman from the South, and their letters went back and forth unknown to everyone but my mother, the postmistress. She was so tight-lipped about post office business that she didn't even mention the situation to my father. Since the blacksmith shop was next door, Orrin could come over to mail a letter or collect one when nobody else was around. I wouldn't be surprised if he and my mother had signals.

But strange things began to happen and the neighbors became suspicious. Why would old Orrin, who lived with his mother, suddenly build a big addition to her house with polished hardwood floors, a kitchen, and a real bathroom? And why would he buy a lot up to the pond and build a little cabin with a screened-in porch on it? And buy two white, wicker rocking chairs for that porch?

Then one day he drove home in a new, sporty blue Chevrolet coupe. Why, when he had that old Model T truck, black and grimy like him? People watched him, and they spied on the few single women in the area, but they couldn't discover a thing.

Then to cap it off, Orrin appeared one morning all cleaned up and in a blue serge suit, white shirt, and tie. Nobody had ever seen him dressed up. Even though his mother had been superintendent of the Sunday School for forty years, Orrin never went to church, so he had no reason to wear anything but the smoky overalls.

The only thing Orrin ever did besides work was pitch horseshoes. Close to the blacksmith shop he had the finest pit in town—white sand from the shore, shiny stakes, and the perfectly balanced shoes he forged. He practiced by the hour between jobs. He played with such concentration, skill, and controlled violence that he had few opponents. Alpheus Hall, who threw the shoes with less force than Orrin, could win a game once in a while. The Williamson boys, who lived on the other side of the blacksmith shop, played as soon as they were big enough. They'd practice while Orrin worked at the forge, and he'd take them on now and then. Sometimes I'd watch from my bedroom window and see a game start right after supper and go on to the dark of a long summer evening. Sometimes I'd go to sleep before a game was finished and then awake with a start when there'd be a great clank as a shoe slammed into a stake.

Once he began building the addition to the house, Orrin practiced less and less. I remember the night that Billy Williamson beat him. Billy was so shocked he couldn't say a word, but Orrin didn't seem to care.

The day he appeared slicked up and in the suit, he started the Chevy, shiny as a copper kettle, and drove off up the road. Old Ada Morris, who had second sight, watched from the post office steps and said, "We'll never see Orrin alive again."

But he was only gone about long enough to drive to Tunk Station, flag down the noon train, and load on his passenger with her luggage. And there she was. They must have found a justice of the peace on the way home, for he introduced tiny, straight, trim Jessica Shelley as his wife. The men decided she didn't have a pretty face, but she wasn't as bad as Beak Alley said when he heard she was from South Carolina: "Couldn't have been anybody between here'n there that would have her."

Beak's wife, Goldie, answered, "There sure wasn't anyone in that distance that would have him."

The neighbors didn't know what to make of the dignified little woman with the southern accent and the strange habits. There were afternoon naps, for instance. The men and women I knew believed that only young children, the aged, the infirm, the seriously ill, and the bone-lazy slept in the daytime. Real people got up at dawn—earlier in the winter—and kept at it until bedtime. The truth is, however, that some women took naps they didn't dare admit to.

Amy Bartlett knew well enough that her sister Hope Williamson slept in the daytime, and because Amy was a big tease, she tried to catch Hope napping. She'd walk in the door and call, "Yoo-hoo! You home, Hope?" and Hope would come running downstairs looking half asleep.

" 'Course I'm home! Where'd I be in the middle of the day but here doing my housework?"

"Did I wake you up?"

"Wake me up? Goodness gracious no! I was straightening up a few bureau drawers before time to start cooking supper."

After several failed attempts at getting a confession from her sister, Amy told the neighbors that Hope must have the neatest bureau drawers in town.

Of course, my mother and all the other busy women had to sit down and rest their feet once in a while. But they would pick up darning, patching, or knitting so they wouldn't be accused of just sitting around.

Into the midst of this Maine work ethic came the new wife. When one of Orrin's cousins said to her in the post office, "I knocked on your door yesterday afternoon. You must have been away. Or were you out picking berries?"

"Mercy, no!" Miss Jessica said in her slow, airy voice. "From one until three I'm sound asleep—cotton balls in my ears, witch hazel packs on my eyes. I wouldn't hear you if you beat the door down. By four I'm bathed and dressed and presentable again."

At four every day I thought she was beautiful, even though some still talked about her less-than-pretty face. Her hair was crimped and fluffed out, she used a little powder and pink rouge on her cheeks, she wore soft, pale dresses of dotted Swiss or flowered dimity, and she smelled faintly of lavender toilet water. In her white shoes and pale stockings she'd walk to the black-smith shop with lemonade and cookies for Orrin, at a time when the tired, sweating village women were cooking supper. Miss Jessica said it didn't seem civilized to dine before seven.

They weren't unkind to her face, but neighbors gathered in little groups outside the store or the post office or the church and shook their heads and clucked their tongues. I heard remarks like, "All foolishness to get a wife the way he did. He should have known . . . "

The secret napper Hope's husband, Walter, said, "I wonder if all southern women lay around all day, or if it's just her?"

"Walter Williamson," Irma Coombs, Orrin's mother, said, "my daughter-in-law's house is kept in excellent order, she's a good cook and a good wife to Orrin. If taking a nap is her way, you just let it be." I was wishing she'd mention that Hope had been napping for years, but Irma was too virtuous to say a thing like that.

As time went on, Miss Jessica had some tongue-clicking to do, too. One day she sighed and said to my mother, "In all my years back home I never heard a man break wind. Gentlemen simply didn't do that in the presence of ladies." She sighed again. "And up here they don't even say 'beg your pardon.' "

From my hiding place I had to cover my mouth to keep from laughing at the thought of the Williamson men, for instance, begging anybody's pardon for an activity they viewed as a competitive sport.

My greatest surprise in this North-South adjustment had to do with black people. We didn't see many—some chauffeurs and maids of summer people, mostly. And I was proud when our young minister said that while Southern people mistreated blacks, we Northerners were more humane.

Then, during the Depression, many white and some black men walked through the village, asking for a day's work to pay for a meal, or searching for a hobo jungle near the railroad tracks. I noticed that many of the neighbors didn't answer when a black man knocked on their doors. "I'm scared of them," Myra Nash said. "Hard telling what they'd do."

Then one day when I was playing by the brook behind Miss Jessica's house I saw a young black man walking slowly by. Miss Jessica came out on the porch and called, "You, boy—come here to me." She handed him a towel and a pan and took him out to the pump where he could wash and cool off. Then she had him sit on the back steps and eat a plate of food. She gave him a clean old pair of Orrin's socks to wear inside his torn shoes, and she didn't even ask him to do any work.

After he left, I walked up to the porch. "You sure were nice to him, Miss Jessica," I said.

"Poor coloreds," she said. "They shouldn't come up here. Northern people never treat them decent."

I was confused after that.

Eventually the neighbors warmed up to Miss Jessica, and I think she grew to accept us, too. We kids liked her before the adults did, though. Perhaps she was homesick sometimes, for she'd come down to the brook where we played, talk to us, and bring us little treats. One day when I was by the brook I got a bad nosebleed. I was scared, and I ran to Miss Jessica's because it was closer than my own. My mother was always nervous about a nosebleed, but Miss Jessica treated it lightly. She gave me a big rag, sat me down with my head tipped back, and pressed a cold spoon to a spot on my neck. "It'll stop in a jiffy," she said. I was never scared of a bloody nose after that.

One day I had run to her house again, and was sitting holding the spoon on my neck while she had gone to the other side of the big kitchen to finish doing her dishes. Orrin, who didn't see me, crept up behind his wife and pinched her bottom. She jumped and giggled, and as she turned to reach up and cuff him with her wet hand, he bent down and gave her a big kiss. She giggled again and pushed him away. "Mr. Orrin! Not before a child!"

Then he saw me and grinned. I don't think I'd ever seen him smile before. And I had never seen any man in our village be so playful with his wife.

All foolishness to get a wife that way? I wasn't so sure.

# My Buddy

I REMEMBER a high school field day, a red Chevrolet coupe with a rumble seat, and Bud Havey. Because I had never been on a high school trip or even ridden in a rumble seat, I was giddy with excitement. I was especially happy to be going in the same car with Bud, yet I feared Miss Belknap would make me ride up front with her. She picked me up first that May morning, and we drove on to Bud's house. The day was perfect—birds, flowers, sunshine, a soft breeze. Bud ran out of his door and said, "Can I ride in the rumble seat, Miss Belknap?"

Gently she corrected him. "May you? Yes, you may." Bud climbed up and opened the back. Then he asked, "Can—may—Glenna ride in here, too?" Miss Belknap scowled and my heart sank. "Well, I don't—" she said. Perhaps it was the perfection of the day or the look on my face that swayed her. Or maybe she just wanted peace and quiet while she drove. Anyway, after a pause she said, "I guess so. Do you want to, Glenna?"

I climbed up quickly, saying, "Oh, yes! Thank you!" Suddenly I didn't care about the field day—I just wanted the ride to last forever. What could be more romantic than riding in a rumble seat with a boy? Perhaps this would be the time when Bud would clasp me in his arms, shower me with passionate kisses, and pledge his undying love. Secretly I had been reading the love magazines that Mama sold in the post office, so I knew all about how it was supposed to go. Bud's reading didn't include pulp love magazines, though, so my scenario didn't occur to him. I try now to remember if he ever did kiss me, but it was so long ago I can't.

Bud and I had been friends all of my freshman year, and we had much in common. We were both only children, we both lived in big old buildings that had once been stores, and we loved to read. I sometimes felt inferior to kids who lived in conventional houses, yet our barn-like dwellings had many hideaways for reading and talking. Often Bud and I challenged the universe, asking ourselves and each other, "Is there really a God? Where is our soul located? Where does it go when we die? Will there always be wars? Why are we so poor and the summer people so rich? What are we supposed to do with our lives?"

We were not always serious, though. Bud loved to collect jokes from magazines, especially *Readers Digest*. He'd read them to me and break into wild laughter before the punch line. He had a funny laugh—almost a cackle. Everyone who heard him had to laugh with him. On the rumble seat we were probably more silly than serious. I kept bouncing up and down and chanting, "We're going to BESTOCCA!" The acronym stood for the activities of the day. B was for baseball. E may have been for elocution, our name then for speaking contests. The S could have been for scholastic tests, which we had taken back in our schools and for which ribbons would be presented at the evening ceremony. T for track. I can't recall the rest. Bud and I rode with Miss Belknap because she had given us elocution lessons and had coached us in the declamations we would present that afternoon. Bud spoke "The Bishop's Candlesticks" from *Les Misérables*, and I gave a cutting from *Anne of Green Gables*. I wanted to do "Gertie Gets Golf," but Miss Belknap called it inane and trivial. At first I hated her choice, but I grew to love it after weeks of her high standards and my slow improvement. I even remember what I wore that day—a white skirt Mama had made and a flowered lavender blouse with puffed sleeves made by my friend Norma's mother, who made one for both Norma and me, and it was my favorite. My hair was so curly that it couldn't be tamed into the current fashion of smooth hair and bangs. After it was whipped by the wind in the rumble seat it was an impossible tangle for the day. Bud's dark curly hair was too short to be messed up.

In mid-morning I sat on the ground with other kids to watch the baseball games. Bud played and I cheered wildly. I can't remember who won. At noon we sat on bleachers and ate the lunches we had brought from home. I probably gave Bud my mother's date-filled cookie and ate his mother's chocolate cake. I loved Bud's laughing, singing mother, and he loved my scowling, worrying one, although he often teased her. On the rare evenings when he could borrow his father's car and drive the seven miles to my place, Mama always sat in the next room with the door open until he left. Even though she was fond of Bud, she felt sure that if she left us alone I'd lose my virtue. She would never have believed that I wanted to be kissed and that he wasn't interested.

Since she didn't want to just tell him to go home, she devised a series of hints, starting at about eight o'clock. The first might be, "Bud, the cat is in for the night. Don't let her out when you leave." He would grin at me and say, "I'll watch out for Daffodil, Kathleen." Then he would wait for the next reminder ten minutes later. "Bud, the milk bottle is between the kitchen door and the screen. Don't kick it over when you go out." "I'll be careful, Kathleen," he'd say, trying not to laugh. The third hint was usually, "Bud, I think Glenna's father has gone to sleep. I surely hope you don't wake him up when you start your car." On that one, he left.

As I sat on the bleachers that noon I suddenly realized how wonderful it was to be young, to be sitting in the sunshine, and to have a friend like Bud. Silly love stories no longer seemed important as I realized I could never live this perfect day again. I started to cry and Bud said, "Hey, what's the matter?" For once I couldn't put my feelings into words. "I've got green grass stains on my skirt," I sobbed. "I'll have to speak my piece in a dirty skirt."

"Oh, that won't show from the stage," he said.

It turned out that both Bud and I were chosen from the afternoon speakers to be part of a small group that spoke in the evening. Some girls from other schools had brought evening gowns in case they were chosen. Evidently Miss Belknap, new to our school, didn't realize her superior abilities as a drama coach and hadn't warned us of the possibility of needing a change of clothes. Thus I spoke in the evening, tangled hair, grass stains, white sneakers, and all. But I didn't care, for Miss Belknap, who seldom gave compliments, told me she was proud of my performance. She left us the next year to teach at Bangor High, and although I competed every year after I never again made the evening finals. When we started home she praised Bud, too, and asked us if we wanted to ride up front where it was warmer. We said, "Oh, no, thanks," and huddled together shivering under the moon and the stars. To paraphrase a line from *Anne of Green Gables*, I was almost completely perfectly happy that night. Again I wanted to cry because soon the day would be gone forever. I would have been surprised then to know that even at my age now, I can relive much of the day.

After high school Bud and I went to different colleges, fell in love with other people, and married them. Soon at his home there were four little girls, at my home three little boys. For a few years we exchanged Christmas cards and family pictures. Then we lost track of each other for several decades. I was amazed to answer the phone one night and hear, "Matthew Cuthbert jogged comfortably along the winding road to Bright River Station"—words from that long-ago freshman declamation. Only Bud could know them, for we had spent many hours together practicing our pieces. He called a few more times in the following years, and we had long conversations about our high school days.

Once when I was waiting with friends to cross a street in Portland, a man on a motorcycle—a man with curly white hair—stopped to talk to me. I don't know how Bud recognized me. We were so surprised to see each other that we couldn't think of much to say. Years later, when Bud and I were both divorced and he had remarried, he sent me a newsletter that he circulated every month to his children and grandchildren. I could sense his love for family by the remarks he made about each member, and about his younger brother who had been born when he was in college. I wasn't surprised that the letter included jokes copied from magazines. The white-haired grampy wasn't so different from the high school freshman.

Still later, when I was seventy-five or older, I found in a box of my father's keepsakes a Sullivan High graduation program in which Ellen Hall, Bud's mother, had played the piano and had sung a solo. On an impulse I sent it to the last address I had for Bud. A few weeks later I received a note from his wife. Bud had been close to death when my note arrived, but he was pleased with the reminder of his mother as a young girl. His passing touched me deeply—surprising since we had had so few contacts through the years. But I had always known that he was out there somewhere, the only other person who would remember that rumble seat ride on a May night.

# Empress Eugenie's Hat

WHEN I FIRST saw them in the Sears Roebuck catalog I wanted one. Then when they appeared in the window of the Five and Dime Store in Ellsworth, my yearning grew. Some of the other girls in grammar school wanted them, too, but money was scarce in the 1930s, and our fathers would consider it all foolishness to spend a couple or three dollars for a hat with a feather. Our mothers, who might understand our feelings, also knew that for that kind of money they could buy many yards of cloth for nightdresses, school dresses, housedresses, or aprons. So I was surprised when on one of our infrequent trips to Ellsworth Mama said I could try on an Empress Eugenie hat.

Mama always had a tiny income from selling magazines, newspapers, and cards in the big old barn of a room where she ran the post office, but she was seldom tempted to spend her money on foolish fads. I was amazed when she agreed to buy me a hat, and even more amazed when she tried some on, too. I think she was disappointed that she couldn't find one big enough to pull down over her mound of thick hair. They fit me perfectly, though, and I loved the feeling as one nestled over my thatch of frizzy curls. I loved the rich shades of royal blue, deep purple, and garnet. And most of all I loved the long feather that curled around and tickled my neck. When I looked at myself in the mirror I forgot my scrawny neck, gangling legs and arms. I felt really grown-up—almost as grown as the high school girls. As a matter of fact, I thought I looked quite interesting.

I waited impatiently to appear in church the next Sunday and show off my hat. And I wasn't the only one who had acquired a

Eugenie hat that week. Mrs. Porter, who had a weather-beaten face and wore faded percale dresses and aprons all week while she did the housework and milked the cows—even she was wearing a purple Eugenie with her good flowered rayon dress. I was glad to see that her hat changed her as much as mine did me, for she looked like the dowager queen from my fairy tale book. And Letitia Hale, a pretty rosy-cheeked high school girl I admired, was wearing a black Empress Eugenie hat that transformed her into a mysterious and glamorous international spy, a femme fatale. After that I kept going to church eagerly to see who had a new Eugenie. Nobody seemed resentful that several other women were wearing identical hats. In fact, I felt I belonged to a large sisterhood; I was one of the many who were finding a new identity in a feathered hat.

As far as I know, none of us wondered much about Empress Eugenie herself. She could have been real or fictional, saint or sinner, for all we cared. Years later in a history class I learned about her, and noted that she died in July of 1920, less than a month after I was born. I also learned that she was an auburn-haired beauty, and as the daughter of a Spanish grandee, of sufficient standing to appear at court balls. Louis Napoleon became smitten with her, and although her standing wasn't impressive enough to make her a desirable wife for an emperor of France, he decided that she would be his mistress. She refused that offer, however, saying she'd be his wife or nothing. It's a pity the women of my village couldn't have known about her. They would have been tickled pink that she kept her virtue intact and got her man in the end. I also learned that, although Eugenie was sometimes willful and impatient, she was as wise, intelligent, and brave as she was beautiful. Three times during her husband's long absences she ruled France as a regent, her knowledge of governmental and religious matters and her courage in the face of the approaching revolution influencing those in high places.

At the collapse of the Empire she fled to England, and later, when widowed, became friends with Queen Victoria, another widow. I thought Marie Eugenie, Empress of France, was wonderful. I was glad she'd worn a hat like mine.

Sometimes, remembering how I felt in that hat, I creep into a store having a half-price sale, and when nobody is looking I try on hats and stare at myself in the mirror. Recently I gazed long at a baseball cap covered with black sequins, and I tried a yellow cloth number with a huge, floppy brim that made me look like a drooping tulip on a very thick stem. The thing is, I never wear hats anywhere except in my yard, to prevent sunstroke. But I almost bought a black straw with a large red rose on the front. It would have added class to my dooryard wanderings, and given my neighborhood kids a good laugh. But it didn't quite make it. My favorite hat, second to the Eugenie, was made of long black and white feathers that felt wonderfully festive. However, I suspect that it made me look like a large and impressive Barred Rock hen. It was a great creation, but not magic. And that was back in the 1940s.

But I'll keep looking. Somewhere there must be one more hat for me—one that will weave that old Empress Eugenie spell.

# My Mother, the Stranger

I LOVED MY MOTHER, Kathleen Proctor
Johnson, and I know she loved me; yet there was always a great
distance between us, a gap created partly by years. Although all
mothers and daughters are a generation apart, we seemed to be
separated by two or three lifetimes. When Kathleen was a baby,
her teenaged mother, Eva, left her in the care of a much older
father, Dana Proctor, and his frail and reclusive mother, Sarah
Knight. Because they lived on a remote farm Kathleen had no
playmates. She loved her Grammie Knight and spent much time
alone with her, accepting her standards for how to behave.
Kathleen believed that a young girl should be quiet and dainty,
and that she should spend her spare time sewing quilt squares and
embroidering. She couldn't understand why her only child—me—
a big clumsy girl, liked to play in mud puddles and climb trees.

Kathleen graduated from Eastern State Normal School in
Castine, where she at last had the companionship of young
women. She loved those years, but I believe her background and
her reserve kept her from forming close relationships.

She met my father, Seth Johnson, when both accepted teaching positions in Winn, in Penobscot County. They were so serious and distant that I marvel they ever got together. From the
little that she told me, their courtship consisted of Sunday afternoon walks. At the end of the year they were married and
moved to Gardiner where Seth could make more money in a
shoe factory. Kathleen kept house in their little apartment, but
had no chance to form friendships with women. When she realized she was pregnant she had no idea what to expect and no

friend to rely on. She asked Seth to take her back to the family farm in Lincolnville where she would be well cared for by the old family doctor who had delivered her. Seth worked on the farm with Dana while they waited for the June day when I was born—the worst day of my mother's life.

When labor started she didn't know what was happening, and her fragile grandmother was as frightened as she was. Seth and Dana went to the village for the doctor. He examined Kathleen, said nothing would happen for a long time, and went outside with Dana and Seth. When they came in to dinner Kathleen was terrified and in agony. She heard her grandmother beg the doctor to help her, and she heard him say, "Women are supposed to suffer." The men went back to the fields until suppertime. Kathleen feared she would die as the day wore on. Later the pain became so intense she prayed for death. I think it was late in the night when I was born—a big baby finally separated from my small mother. She would never have admitted to herself that she resented me for causing all that horror, but I always thought she did.

I loved learning and was often a noisy show-off, belting out poetry at the top of my lungs. My mother's advice was a quotation: "Be good, sweet maid, and let who will, be clever." She never defined "being good," but I assumed it meant being shy, modest, and obedient. Nobody had talked to her about sex and she had no words for me except, "Remember there are some mistakes a girl need make but once," and "You will never get a husband if you tarnish your reputation." Although I was often thoughtless, my behavior was never really bad. Yet I remember my mother's expression for disapproval: a wrinkling of her forehead, a pursing of her lips, and a shake of her head.

I believe now that Kathleen must have led a lonely life. When my father was in the house, he preferred reading a book to talking with his wife. The Masonic orders were the love of his life, and although Kathleen attended the Eastern Star, running

*Glenna's parents, Kathleen and Seth Johnson, pictured here in 1917*

the post office six days a week kept her from women's clubs and church groups. I wonder if she felt that her young mother, who loved dancing, bridge, and pretty clothes, and her daughter, who loved dancing, swimming, and skating, led happier lives than she did.

I wish that I had listened more carefully to my mother, for her upbringing rooted in an earlier century gave her a perspective on the twenties and thirties that was wise and sensible. She conserved everything when it wasn't popular to do so, and she valued old family possessions when the prevailing mode was to throw them on the dump and buy new furnishings and dishes from Sears and Roebuck. She did home cooking and preserving long after canned, packaged, and frozen foods became the vogue. She renovated old clothes instead of buying new house-dresses from Newberry's. She kept her hair long and did it up Gibson-Girl style, rather than getting a stylish bob and a permanent. I doubt she ever owned lipstick or nail polish. I grew up thinking she was hopelessly old-fashioned.

I did, however, admire her for her goodness. She was always kind to my grandmother, her mother-in-law, who became demanding as she grew older. Mama never failed to help her own mother who had deserted her. She sewed for families in need and she sent many suppers to Aunt Tune and other feeble old women who had no relatives. Yet I'm not sure whether she was aware of her virtues or whether she saw herself as a misfit.

One day in the hospital shortly before her death my mother asked me to read a book to her. I read the entire book, a quiet story about life on the coast. I would have liked to talk about serious matters, but neither of us could break a lifetime habit. After her death I received a note from an acquaintance. She wrote, "I wish I could have gotten to know Kathleen. I wish we could have been friends." She expressed my feelings exactly.

At her funeral the minister said, "Kathleen often had a little half-smile that seemed to say she knew a secret beyond the grasp of the rest of us."

That may have been the truth. I wish I knew.

# Part II

My busiest years were often my happiest, despite problems that I couldn't handle. In Aroostook, my husband, Don, and I lived and worked on the farm and tended with pride our three sons. We both eventually taught at Easton High School and later at Presque Isle High School. I directed school plays, and Don coached sports teams. Keeping up with the boys' school activities and athletic teams was our social life.

Although I liked all the things I was doing, I never got organized, and I lived with a guilty conscience. If I were doing housework I felt I should be correcting papers; if I were doing schoolwork I wanted to be cooking something special. I had neither time nor energy to consider where my life was heading or to know what was going on in the world—that is, until the Vietnam War hit home for my family. I just tore into each day's schedule and fell into bed exhausted at night. Sometimes I daydreamed that when I grew old and retired I'd sleep at least fifteen hours a night, waking up only to eat and now and then read a good book. I look back and wish I had been a better-organized farm wife, a wiser mother, a more creative teacher. Still, there are many, many good memories from those years.

*Don Smith and Glenna Johnson at the Phi Eta Kappa fraternity house at the University of Maine at Orono, c. 1939*

*Glenna gets set to snowshoe on a winter day in Presque Isle.*

# Tell Me the Landscape

FOR NEARLY SEVEN decades the geography of Aroostook County has become a part of me. Now, after reading *Dakota: A Spiritual Geography,* by poet Kathleen Norris, I see more clearly my changes. Norris prefaces her work with the quotation, "Tell me the landscape in which you live and I will tell you who you are." (José Ortega y Gasset)

I grew up on the coast of Maine in a cozy village with houses nestled together, protected by a low hill and many ancient trees. Then, in 1941, I, as a new farm wife, moved to The County, a land with massive, silent, empty spaces. Although I felt at home with the people I met, it took several years for me to be comfortable with the place.

First I learned to admire the big sky—the giant, inverted bowl that fits snugly over almost flat fields and gentle hills. Sometimes when I see a potato field that rolls right up to the sky, I believe that if I walked across that field I could see the whole world. On my early morning rides to the schoolhouse where I taught in those new years, I noticed the colors: cold pewter gray, bright Wedgwood blue, and sometimes a carnival glass riot of orange, gold, and red as the winter morning sun splashed the snow and the sky. As a child I stared at the bay; in Aroostook I stared at the sky and learned to love its moods.

It took me longer to accept the empty stretches. In fact, I didn't realize how much they were a part of me until years later when I was thinking of retiring and moving back to the coast. Yet always when I came home from a visit downstate, the wide vistas of fields welcomed me as I drove north of Houlton. I even imagined that there was more good air here—that breathing was easier. I take the time to watch and breathe—and I have learned to live in harmony with the dramatic changes of the seasons: the quick leap from snowbanks to potato planting, the soft greens of early spring, the miles of flower gardens when the potatoes blossom, the crisp fall when giant mechanized insects crawl over the brown earth.

I still have a love-fear relationship with winter. When the weatherman tells me it's twenty-below with a wind chill of minus-forty, I huddle close to the stove, my only problem being to stay warm. Or if I must start my creaking, cold car and keep an appointment or buy groceries, I see myself as a puny thing in a spluttering little metal box, trying to show off before God. I used to fear the days and nights when the swirling snows made an arctic wilderness of our farm, when the plows were conquered, when I couldn't leave home, and nobody else could come in. Yet at some point through the years I began to feel reborn in this isolation. As a captive in a cold, white world I could take a long look at my place and the people in it.

One night when I was a young wife, a group of us walked on the crusted snow from Easton to Easton Center. We sang and laughed as the moon made shadows on shining snow-mountains. For a few hours, we ordinary farm people and our ordinary routines ceased to exist.

Sometimes at the farm I'd go outdoors on a cold night and look at the stars. I'd listen to the silence and to a humming I couldn't define. I fancied it must be angels singing. I'd lie in the snow, spread my arms, and make an angel, just in case one might be looking down.

In some ways a blizzard is like the ocean of my childhood; both are fearsome and beautiful, and both jolt me to an awareness of my world. For many months winter dictates the rhythms of my life. Then in April I am delighted again to see the drifts shrink, to hang my washing outdoors on the line, to hunt for crocus blossoms and then fiddleheads, and to see young parents taking babies out in strollers—babies who are seeing their first springtime.

In Aroostook, it took me longest of all to love the winds. The stiff breezes back home on the coast rattled the chimney, blew the dry leaves down the street, and embarrassed us girls by flipping our skirts into the air. But they were generally tame winds, reined in by the tall trees and the hill. On the farm, though, the gale howled across barren fields and hit the buildings with such ferocity that it rattled the windows, tore at the shingles, and snapped at the foundations. Then it would turn tricky and be calm for a minute, only to gather such force that I would be sure the windows would break, the chimney would fall down, or the shed roof would fly away.

And that wasn't the worst of my fear. If I were alone in the house I'd huddle shivering by the fireplace, sure that something or someone was banging on the door, creaking up the cellar stairs, or dragging across the shed chamber. Finally one night, angry at my cowardice, I went outdoors without a lantern and walked all the way around the buildings. Although my heart was pounding, nothing jumped out of the shadows. I was alone with the flying clouds, the stars, and the wind. That night was the beginning of my conquering my fears, yet after I still played the radio at top volume, trying to drown the mournful sounds. I can't remember exactly when the wind became my night music as I read, or when it became my earth mother, lulling me to sleep at bedtime, waking me softly in the morning.

It has been a slow process, me becoming Aroostook. Sometimes I wonder what my life would be in another place. Although I resist change, I believe I adapt fairly well to new situations when I have to. I could be content in Portland, Maine, or Portland, Oregon. Still, call me provincial, call me an old fogy— I hope I never find out who I'd be outside The County.

# Learning Together

SOMEWHERE THERE MIGHT have been
someone as scared as I was when I faced my first class, but I
doubt it. I knew I wasn't a teacher, and I suspected the students
soon would know it. In the summer of 1941 I had left my snug
coastal village to become a wife and to live on a potato farm. I
knew I had much to learn, and I looked forward to the long winter for the learning and adjusting. But I hadn't reckoned on the
knock on my door in late summer.

The superintendent of schools for Fort Fairfield and Easton
introduced himself and said that he had several classrooms without teachers, and since I had a college degree he could get me
certified. I assured him that I had no knowledge of how to teach
grammar school, and besides, I was busy where I was. He
brushed away my protests, and asked if I would like the seventh-
and eighth-grade room in town or one of the rural schools.

My husband and I knew we could use the money (about
thirty dollars a week), so I decided on the grammar school in
town. I wanted to choose the one-room schoolhouse near the
farm, but I was scared of keeping the wood fire going. I imagined that I would either burn down the schoolhouse or let the
fire go out and freeze the kids.

I asked the superintendent for plans and methods for teaching
seventh- and eighth-grade subjects, and he said none existed.
"Just visit the room and look over the books," he said. And after
that, when he visited to bring paper and supplies, I would deluge
him with questions. He would pat me on the shoulder and say,

"You're doing just fine," and tell me about his racehorse. So I learned along with the kids.

The old square building on the hill above Easton village held the three high school rooms upstairs and two rooms downstairs: one for the fifth and sixth grades, and one for seventh and eighth grades. My room smelled of floor oil, dust, and mice. The books were dull and worn, and although I'd always loved school, I could find little of interest between those faded covers. However, if I read every night I could keep a day ahead of the kids in all subjects but eighth-grade arithmetic. The problems were impossible: "How tall is the tree if the shadow is cast in the river where the boat is going upstream at ten miles an hour? And when will the boat reach Albany?" They made no sense to me. Luckily my new husband was good at math, and he agreed to teach me enough each night to get me through the next day. The Lord help me if a pupil got interested and worked ahead in the book. The prevailing teacher technique was never to admit to a student that you didn't know an answer. One should say, "Look it up yourself and then you'll remember it." I felt that if the kids had any brains at all it would take them about two weeks to learn that I didn't know anything, so I decided to be honest with them. I would answer their questions with, "I don't know, but let's see if we can find out."

On that first terrifying day I saw before me a handful of girls—gentle, quiet Lucille, Helen, Christine, the O'Blenes girls, and others that I've forgotten—who were willing to work hard for the teacher. I liked them right away. But three-fourths of the seats were filled with boys—grinning, wriggling, loud ones. I didn't understand boys that age. I had no brothers, and I had feared most of the boys when I was in grammar school. But I blundered along. While I was meeting with one class the members of the other were supposed to be doing their assignments. However, the brightest ones would finish their work and look for more interesting pursuits.

One day early in the year the seventh-grade boys planned an all-out war. They brought their peashooters to school, and came armed with pockets full of dried peas, beans, and corn. While I was busy with the eighth-grade lessons the missiles began to fly. They didn't aim at me or at the other students; their targets seemed to be points on a map on the wall, probably the enemy countries, for we all felt the horrors of the war. Anyway, by noon there were enough vegetables on the floor to make a good-sized stew. Yet I hadn't been able to catch even one culprit. I said nothing because I had no idea how to deal with the situation.

At the end of the day I dismissed the eighth-graders, and I told the seventh-graders that anyone who had not used a weapon could leave, too. I felt sure that the girls had not joined in the battle; all day I could sense their disgust at the boys. I added that if anyone left who had done some shooting, I would not be responsible for that person's safety on the playground the next day. The girls filed out and one boy rose to follow them. A low rumble from the other boys caused him to return to his seat, however.

My husband did some coaching after school, and I often worked in my classroom until five or after, until he picked me up. So I told the seventh-graders that they would remain until I left, and during that time they would write without stopping, "I will not bring a peashooter to school again. Shooting peas can be dangerous." I gave each a stack of paper, instructing them to practice their penmanship while they were at it. They got to work with no protest. I had learned that I could trust these kids to have a sense of honesty and fair play. Finally one boy said, "My arm aches from writing."

I said, "That's too bad, but think how much worse you would feel if you had accidentally hit someone with a pea. Keep writing."

Don was especially late that night. The boys awaited him eagerly; yet a couple of them cleaned the boards and erasers before they left (this was a volunteer chore, not a duty), and they all gave a friendly grin and said good-night—tall Albert, blond Dick, the two Waynes, Pop, Alan, and others.

Although the boys were an hour late for supper, I received no complaints from parents. "You punish him in school and I'll give him twice as much punishment at home" was the prevailing attitude. Alan's mother said that he came home so mad at himself that he broke his peashooter into little pieces, threw it on the floor, and stamped on it before he ate his supper. But I saw none of his anger. The son of the high school principal, Alan had been taught to respect school and teachers, even such a one as I.

There was one thing I didn't like during my late, quiet afternoons in the room: mice from the basement would come up and visit the big wicker wastebasket where we all threw the scraps from our dinner kettles. There was one boy who daydreamed through his classes, and remained after school to finish his work. He'd hurry through the lessons so he could kick the basket and catch mice as they ran out. I think "basket-mouse" was his favorite game.

Redheaded George and tall Arnold, eighth-graders who sat in the back row, were bright and quick with their studies. When they had nothing to do they would hide a magazine—often *Reader's Digest*—inside their biggest books and read the jokes. I knew what they were up to when I saw their grins, for there was nothing to smile about in those old geography books. I was glad to have them reading magazines, but since the practice would have been frowned upon at the time, I didn't ever catch them in the act.

Each morning after the flag salute, Bible reading, and the Lord's Prayer, I read from a book for a half-hour. The kids enjoyed that, but after the pea-shooting episode I decided to keep their hands busy while they listened. So I taught them to knit.

Most of the girls could knit, and they helped teach the boys. Also, mamas and grammies, who donated the knitting needles and yarn scraps, did some instructing at night. Sometimes a student would drop a stitch, and while I repaired it for them, they'd take over reading to the class. We had all agreed to make squares of the same size, and I promised to sew them together into afghans to donate to the Red Cross. As the students got interested in the project, they competed to see who could make the most squares. One day several of them declared that Wendell (called Pop) was cheating because his grandmother Myra finished his square every night and started another for him. I assured them that since we were making the afghans for a good cause, they should accept help wherever it was offered. One day the superintendent dropped in during the knitting and reading time. He said he saw it, but he wasn't sure he believed it. Perhaps then he wished that he had taken the time to instruct me in more conventional teaching methods.

With a little shrinking of some and stretching of others, the squares went together surprisingly well, and we were all proud to see one of the afghans displayed in the bank building before it was sent off.

Although I tried to be conscientious about teaching the contents of the books, I was as glad as the kids were to take a break from the routine. One day an enormous white owl landed on the nearby peak of Ralph White's barn roof. We all stood quietly at the windows and watched the dignified creature until at last he spread his wings and flew away. Then we looked him up in the encyclopedia.

As the year went on, the students asked to do more unconventional things. We had baseball spelling matches, and we played word games. And at some point I developed the bad habit of stalling for time when they made a request so I could think about whether or not it was a good thing to do. I would say, "We'll see. It may depend upon how well your work is done, and how you act." One day George and Arnold said they had prepared a skit, and I said they could perform it. One of them was a perfect imitation of me and the other was a student. I can remember only the opening. "Student: Do you think the sun will come up tomorrow? Teacher: It depends on how you act." It was a witty skit, and we all had a good laugh over it.

Soon it was time to plan eighth-grade graduation. The tradition was to decorate the stage of the Grange Hall down in the village, where students would recite poems and speak pieces. But this class decided that they'd like to write a play. Starting with the idea of George and Arnold's skit, they wrote a satire of schools, students, and teachers. We had fun doing it, and the parents laughed when they watched it.

On the last day of school I was unprepared for the gifts the students brought me—thoughtful household items chosen and wrapped by mothers who seemed to forgive me my lacks as a teacher. After the students left, I put my head down on the desk and cried. I knew then that I wanted to learn to be a good teacher, and yet I must have realized that no matter how many classes I might face in the future, none would live in my memory with the shine of this first one.

I've lost track of many of them, but some I've seen through the years. Paul, Perley, Wayne, and Earl were my colleagues in the Presque Isle school system. When I see Paul, I often remember that I told him he would never make it through high school because his handwriting was so careless. When he earned his master's degree from the University of Maine, I admitted to him that I was wrong. I'll always remember Perley for reaching his right hand behind his head and scratching his left ear when he was searching for an answer. Wayne was a jolly boy, but yet a serious reader. Earl was a serious student, yet very strong and outdoorsy. Milford grew up to be a banker. I saw Helen and Christine become mothers and then grandmothers. Helen travels, paints, and sings in a choir. Christine is a social worker.

Marvin's granddaughter was in one of my classes in Presque Isle. She was incredulous when I told her I had taught her grandfather in school; she didn't think anybody could be that old. I have outlived some of the 1941 seventh- and eighth-grade students. Arnold was killed in a car accident soon after he graduated; George died of a stroke—a brilliant young lawyer with a wife and four young children.

Yet in some treasured corner of my mind we are all still there in the dusty old room with the mouse-inhabited wastebasket, playing some good-natured pranks on each other, learning together a few facts from the old books, and realizing, again together, that if teacher and students like and trust each other, sometimes good things will happen.

# Butchie

BECAUSE MY MEMORY of my middle years is
sketchy, I needed to have a relative remind me of how Butchie
became part of our family. I was sure, however, that we did not
go to a pet store or an animal shelter to choose a pet. It never
worked that way.

The pattern started when we were newly married. A friend of
my mother's from down on the coast said she was going to give
me her cat Snooty because she was moving into a complex
where pets were not allowed.

"Glenna and her husband live way up there in Aroostook with
all that empty space, so they'd love to have Snooty, I know," she
told Mama.

That same way of thinking brought us what one woman—
identity now unknown—called her rare Abyssinian guinea pig.
She said she'd be traveling and that she'd come back to get it in
a few months. She never did. And then there were the people
who dropped off the golden monkey. There were also donations
of ducks, rabbits, and a parakeet. One day a station wagon drove
by and someone threw a cat on our lawn. That poor kitty must
have been mistreated in other ways, too, for she never did trust
people. I seem to recall a tall man, an acquaintance of my husband, coming to the door one evening and handing us a pup.
But that one was not Butchie.

My sister-in-law Natalie visited one day when our oldest son,
Steve, was a baby. "Stevie needs a pup," she said.

Don and I assured her that we'd get a dog later when Steve
was older. A few days later Natalie brought Butchie and gave him

to Steve, who loved him instantly. Then Nat smiled and said, "If you want to take the pup away from him, I'll take it back."

Actually, I never felt that we owned Butchie, for he was entirely his own man. Or I guess I should say his own dog, although his thinking seemed more human than canine. We did make an effort to train him, but it was like teaching a brook not to run downhill. Butchie was a constant. There were no leash laws on a farm road in the forties, and I can't remember that people had their pets spayed or neutered, so Butchie's favorite occupation was visiting the homes of lady dogs in heat. Sometimes he'd be away for several days, and we would drive around back roads and call his name. When we were all sad that we would never see him again, he'd come trotting across the field, wagging his tail. We would shake our fingers at him and say, "Have you been chasing girls again?" Then he would hang his head and grin. I have never seen another dog with such an engaging, sheepish grin.

A man on another road had a prize dog from whom he planned to raise expensive pups. He told us that he would keep Butchie away from his dog if it was the last thing he did. When his dog was in heat, the man locked her in the house all day and in the garage at night. Evidently, Butchie observed the pattern from a distance, because one day he hid in the garage and was there waiting when his ladylove was locked up for the night. Butchie had his way with her and in due time she produced a litter of mongrel pups. We were grateful that the dog owner turned out to be a good sport about the misdeed.

One day Butchie returned battered and lame from several days of courting. When he limped to the door we all petted him with cries of "Oh, poor Butchie!" He liked the sympathy so much that thereafter he contrived to get it by assuming a limp when he thought he was in sight of the house.

Then when he had perfected his act he took it on the road. In his travels he had learned that Steve went to "training school," seven miles away in Presque Isle. One day he jogged out to the school, waited until recess, and started his limping and crying. Steve telephoned to ask me to come out to get the dog. He said, "My teacher will keep him in our room until you get here." I arrived to find Butchie basking in pats and sympathy from dozens of kids and the teacher. On the way home I said, "Butchie, you are a big faker." He pounded his tail on the seat, gave me the grin, and enjoyed his ride. Then he bounded out of the car on all fours and ran off in search of other adventures. He tried the school scam a few more times before the teachers caught on.

He found other ways to con us, too. I fed him sensibly night and morning, yet he worked out his own food plan. One day brother-in-law Ken Kilpatrick said, "Why don't you ever feed Butchie? Usually he comes to our house at eleven, just as we sit down to dinner. He's so hungry we have to feed him." June, my mother-in-law, was amazed to hear that. "We always feed Butchie at eleven-thirty," she said. "Poor thing comes in just starved to death while we're eating." Later when Don and I told that story to our friends, the Jewells, they burst out laughing. "We always feed him at twelve," they said. "We've been planning to send you our bill." Knowing how kindhearted all those people were, I was sure that Butchie was getting generous helpings of cookies and doughnuts along with good food. We wondered if there were still other kitchens where he put on the starvation act. But because he traveled so many miles a day he didn't get fat.

When on a Saturday night Don and I would go to a movie at Fort Fairfield, a number of miles away, we'd tell the boys and the sitter to keep Butchie in the house so he wouldn't chase us. But Butchie would find a way to get out, and if we had left a car window open he'd be sleeping in the backseat when the movie ended.

Although we took him with us on family outings, he seemed to enjoy the ride best when he'd chased us to our destination.

Although Butchie always did as he pleased, he had a good idea of what was going on in the family, and he was loyal. One summer we were having a hard time with a weasel that was stealing eggs from the hen pen. When Don was home and ready to deal with him, the weasel didn't show himself. When next he appeared Butchie would bark and drive him away, but as soon as the dog left on a trip the creature would come back. Finally, one day, Butchie cornered him in the niche where the chimney met the wall. The two were evenly matched and fought hard, scratching and snarling. When they'd tire, the weasel would back into his corner and Butchie would guard him until they started another battle. Without Don there, I wondered if I should go out with a broom and chase the weasel away so Butchie wouldn't get hurt. Yet I sensed that Butchie wanted to handle the situation, so I watched from the window. At last he got the tired weasel by the neck and shook him until he died. Then he sat down beside the body. I went out and praised him, but he refused to budge until Don came home to supper. Then, after being told again that he was a wonderful dog, he trotted off and allowed Don to dispose of the body. After that he saw himself as our protector against all wild animals, and one by one he killed rabbits and three little skunks we'd found in the road after their mother had been run over. (The little skunks had previously had their moment of fame, however. In the Parade of Pets at the Recreation Center, my son, Barney, carried them in a potato basket labeled, THREE SCENTS, and they won a blue ribbon.)

I remember little about most of the pets that came to us. Neither the rare Abyssinian guinea pig nor the golden monkey were enjoyable pets. Rare Pig had hair so long he looked like a dust mop, and he didn't move much. My only clear memory of him is that he liked to eat lettuce, and that I had to move the hair to see which end to feed. The monkey was beautiful, but he hissed and snarled at us most of the time. I hated it that every time I played the piano he put his little hands over his ears and screamed. It's true that I wasn't a great player. One day we were visited by a young woman who loved rare animals. She said she wished she had the pair, and we gave them to her quickly, before she could change her mind.

I often think of Butchie, though—he was family. As he aged he didn't slow down in his travels, but finally he became ill. We intended to take him to the vet, but a young airman, a medic who lived in an apartment we rented out, took him to the hospital at Loring where he had a growth removed by a surgeon. The airman said the hospital would keep Butchie a few days to be sure there were no complications. The next day, however, he eluded his benefactors and ran home, a distance of more than twenty miles.

His health was good for some time after that, but he was getting old. Finally he crawled away and died beside the road—our little wanderer's favorite place. Steve and his friend Dana found him, and knowing how sad Steve's little brothers, Barney and Mel, would be if they saw him, they buried him. That was fitting, for he had come to us as Stevie's pup.

Years before, on the day the picture was taken, we had arranged with a photographer to come to the farm in the afternoon to take a Christmas portrait. When Steve got home from school he put on his blue pajamas to be ready for the picture. Barney had a cold and had been in bed all day with a fever. I got him up in his red Dr. Dentons just long enough for the picture taking. Mel woke up happy from his nap in his yellow sleepers. The fireplace logs were burning brightly, and as the photographer arranged our sons and set up his equipment I was overcome with thankfulness that three such wonderful little boys were in

*Glenna's sons (from left to right), Mel, Steve, and Barney, and their dog, Butchie, who decided at the last moment to pose with the boys*

my care and keeping. Then there was a scratch on the door. Butchie came in, looked at the photographer and at the boys, and established himself front and center, his head cocked.

"Is he going to be in the picture?" the photographer asked.

"I guess he plans to be," I said.

I've always loved the picture, yet it sometimes makes me sad to look at my sons and remember how quickly the busy, happy days of their childhood sped by. Then I look at Butchie, and I have to smile.

# The New Hudson

WHEN, IN 1941, I married Don Smith and moved
to an Aroostook potato farm, I learned that since no errand was
within walking distance, a car was a necessity. For a while we
couldn't afford a new one, but we made do with old clunkers
kept on the road by brother-in-law Kenneth. A skilled
mechanic, Ken could make any motor purr if it had even one
purr left in it.

Although they were temperamental, some of our old heaps
were interesting. There was the ancient Packard inherited from
Don's grandfather, Cal Smith. It must have been grand in its day,
but in our day it shook and rattled so much that the windows
kept breaking. This was not a good thing in below-zero weather
in a car with no heater.

Because Don was teaching and coaching there, we drove to
Mars Hill one cold night to watch a basketball game. An Easton
boy, Morrison Cumming, rode with us because he wanted to see
his girlfriend, pretty Mary Hamilton. On the ride home he was
sitting in the backseat beside a broken window. When Don
asked the unnecessary question, "Are you cold, Morrison?" He
grinned and answered through chattering teeth, "Oh, no,
Donnie!" Had I been able to see the future on that cold ride, I
would have been warmed by the long and loving marriage of
Morrison and Mary, by the many times I had heard them laugh,
and by memories of their big and happy family.

For all its faults, that long gray Packard had one advantage in
winter: It was so heavy that if Don drove fast enough he could
plow through new snow on his way to school. One neighbor

along the way said he didn't dare drive onto the road until he saw Don go barreling by.

Then there was the car we called "the pink one," a venerable Nash that had lost many of its abilities, but had retained its glossy bright pink exterior. Never a man's car, surely. I hoped that years earlier it had been the pride of a lovely lady. Our teaching jobs at the time were in different towns, so when my husband and I were lucky enough to have two old cars that would start in the morning, Don would always say, "You take the pink one."

Thus we kept going, grateful that Ken would leave his warm bed, climb into his wrecker, and tow us from where we had broken down.

Then came the war and restricted availability of new cars. Besides our failing jalopies, we had only an old farm truck, which would lose its brakes going downhill with a load of potatoes on, the driver frantically grinding gears in an attempt to slow down.

Since the area was running out of decent secondhand cars we were forced to sign up for a new one. We were at the end of a long list of equally needy rural people trying to run farms with rationed gas, increased government regulations, and obsolete farm machinery. Cars dribbled into the dealer one at a time, and we had to take whatever came in when it was our turn or go back to the end of the line. We hoped our car would be on the low end of the price range. Still, our current car was a slate-gray Studebaker. We were told the gray was a primer coat. It never did have a glossy surface. It was so badly rusted that from the driver's seat I could look down and see the gravel of the road. We knew we'd take the new car no matter what. Finally, Frank Hayes called and said our car was ready for us.

Oh, when we saw it! At a cost of about nine hundred or so dollars, it was the top of the Hudson luxury line: two-tone brown in color, white sidewalls, front- and backseat radios, a Venetian blind on the back window, and beautiful satin seats in a brownish wine color. The wood on the dashboard was a work of art, and the seats were the most comfortable of any car I'd known or that I've sat in since. The car begged to be polished and pampered, to be saved for Sundays and special occasions; unfortunately, it had to double as a farm vehicle. Before the car was a week old Don bought a calf and brought it home in the backseat. So much for that new-car smell. During digging I transported potato pickers in it morning and night. Often it was piled with broken farm machinery parts needing to go for repair. Yet for all its abuse, the Hudson remained dependable for a good ten years. It was wonderful to visit my parents downstate or go to a basketball tournament in Bangor without breaking down either way.

We loved that Hudson and hated to part with it when it wore out beyond repair. Yet when we went shopping for a second-hand car, all the fates lined up and smiled upon us. Somebody told Don about an old Hudson for sale in Fort Fairfield, owned by a widow who didn't drive it. All winter it was put up on blocks and in summer the lady's son drove her every Saturday afternoon to the grocery store and back. Despite its age, it still had that new-car smell. It was black and had no frills, but it was as dependable as its elegant predecessor, nearly as comfortable, and equally loved by us Smiths. Since by that time we had an old pickup, this Hudson could be a self-respecting car, and it served us well for another decade. If only the company hadn't gone out of business I might still be driving a Hudson.

# War

THE BLACKEST and most fearsome time of my life was the period when our oldest son, Steve, was in Vietnam. I have never been able to deal with the idea of war. Even in school I hated to read about battles and generals who were considered heroes. It seemed to me that as long as we settle our problems by having young people kill each other, we are nothing but bullies and savages. Steve had opted for training that would put him in a medical battalion, and although I was proud of his beliefs and his actions, I still had a hard time justifying the war.

I didn't handle those Vietnam years well. I tried to keep so busy that I wouldn't think about the war. On many nights I would sit up late reading a mystery novel rather than go to bed and think about where Steve was. I didn't even write to him as often as I should have.

From the time he went to basic training Steve seemed to do the best he could in an alien environment. In one letter from Fort Dix in New Jersey, he wrote that their young lieutenant had led them on a march and had gotten lost on a major highway, making them wonder where he would lead them once they got into a jungle.

In his second year of service, Steve made the army basketball team and was stationed in Hawaii, where he did nothing more dangerous than go to practice and play games. But, after that year, he was sent to Vietnam, and inside my throat there was a lump that didn't go away.

When Steve came home on leave before going overseas I couldn't get accustomed to the sight of the uniform hanging there in his room. He put it on the day he left, and we drove him to Houlton, where he said he'd hitchhike back to his post. In his college years he had often hitchhiked long distances, saying he could go anywhere with an apple in one pocket and a paperback in another. I couldn't convince him otherwise. There he stood alone in the road in that uniform. I can never erase that image from my mind. As we drove away I was sure my heart would break.

One day at Presque Isle High School where both my husband and I taught, Don was summoned over the intercom to the office for a phone call. The secretary said it was an emergency and her voice sounded tense and scared. Some of the kids in our son Mel's class at the school, knowing he had a brother in Vietnam, began to cry. I was somewhere in the building, but I didn't hear Don being summoned. Later, Don told me that he was so scared he could hardly breathe as he ran to the office.

When he picked up the phone a neighbor's voice said, "Don, come home quick! Your potato house is on fire and the wind is blowing right toward your house!"

Don laughed and said, "Oh, good! Good!" The neighbor thought Don had lost his mind.

The potato house was a total loss, but fire departments remained all day and saved the house. None of us was greatly upset about the potato house, thinking about what that call could have been.

Months dragged by. After what seemed a century of watching CBS war news, we turned the TV off one night as the telephone rang. I answered and heard Steve's voice. "Will you come and get me?"

"Where are you?" I asked, my heart pounding.

"Here at Presque Isle Airport," he said.

I sat down and cried. Don was as stunned as I was.

We drove the seven miles to the airport, and there was our beloved oldest son, looking like himself and not wounded as far as we could tell.

The very first thing Steve did when he got home was open the refrigerator freezer and take out a half-gallon of ice cream. The next day he asked me if I would cook him some macaroni and cheese. I said, "Oh, no. I'll cook a great meal, steak and—"

"But I'd like some macaroni and cheese," he said.

He never talked much about army food, but one day he said he hoped he'd never have to eat Spam again. When we had a small welcome-home celebration at Ma Dudley's, a local restaurant that served meals family-style, Steve ate serving after serving of the home-cooked chops, chicken, vegetables, salads, and bread. His Uncle Ken joked that Steve had survived Vietnam, but he wondered if he could survive Ma Dudley's.

Later, I learned that on Steve's flight home, servicemen flew standby. On Northeast Airlines from Boston to Presque Isle a meal was served, and Steve was passed over. He was hungry, so he asked the stewardess if he might have lunch. He was told no, lunch was only for the regular passengers. I have often wished I could tell that stewardess how much it hurt me that she refused food to my son and probably to many other servicemen. In some ways we have become more human as life and wars go on. Now we can hate our involvement in a war that seems wrong to us and yet provide respect and kind treatment to returning veterans who were thrust into a war not of their making, and who did the best they could.

# Difficult Questions,
# Precious Memories

SINCE SEPTEMBER 11, I've wondered why I am taking up space when the lives of so many deserving younger people have been destroyed. What can I do? I don't have much money or energy to donate. I can only remember what America has meant to me for nine decades.

I revisit the fifties when my sons were in school, and Don and I were teaching. Especially, I remember our mealtimes. We sat down together for a big breakfast before six o'clock and again for a big supper when we had all returned from after-school activities. I liked cooking for my family. Although we raised and ate many vegetables, today's nutritionists would frown on our amounts of French toast, bacon, steak, homemade doughnuts, and pies. Yet we liked our meals, and we enjoyed each other.

Usually, we came to the table good-natured, even early in the morning. Barney and Mel sometimes performed little skits while we ate. They might be the animals on a cereal box or, from the radio, the Sleepers of Caribou or the weatherman. They loved the Sleepers' ads because the brothers talked fast and often mentioned groceries and clothing in the same sentence. Barney might say, "My brother and I are offering a sale on cucumbers 'n' sneakers today." Mel would add, "This will be a perfect day all over Aroostook, folks, unless it happens to rain." There was laughter; perhaps it helped us digest the big meals.

Even at the table, the boys' constant competing went on and Barney and Mel tried to keep up with older brother Steve. One morning Barney said, "How come Steve has nine prunes, and I

*Glenna and her grown sons at Higgins Beach in Scarborough, Maine*

have only eight?" I was surprised because prunes were far from his favorites. Often there were I-can-eat-more-eggs-than-you battles. I once asked my doctor if I should limit the eggs. He told me to give them all they wanted. Steve commented recently that seven didn't seem an excessive number at the time.

Though we all ate too much at every meal, there were still conflicts about who would get the last chop or ear of corn. These arguments often ended with the most cutting accusation of all: "Remember that time you ate all the ice cream." I can't recall now who the original culprit was—perhaps Steve, for he loved all ice cream except choc-van-straw, which he said I always bought. On the day he returned from Vietnam, he opened the refrigerator, brought out a box of choc-van-straw and asked, "Is this the same ice cream I wouldn't eat before I joined the army?"

Mel says that at supper we never had normal conversations. Rather, we all wanted to jump in and tell our own stories. Even so, by the end of the meal we all knew how everybody's day had gone. Mel also recalls that Don and I talked endlessly about school, and I remember that Steve and I often talked about a book we'd both read. One night Barney, tired of this adult fare, gave a review of *The Adventures of Timothy Turtle*, complete with wild symbolism and deep meanings. He ended by declaring that all of Timothy's woes came from heredity or environment, and that his parents were to blame either way. We all had a good laugh, yet I took seriously the implied rebuke in his satire. I did talk too much.

One night Mel brought a copy of *Boys' Life* to the table and read a joke: "Unfortunately, a man fell out of an airplane. Fortunately, he wore a parachute. Unfortunately, the parachute didn't open. Fortunately, he was headed for a haystack. Unfortunately, there was a pitchfork in the haystack. Fortunately, he missed the pitchfork. Unfortunately, he missed the haystack, too."

Mel started giggling at the end of the first sentence and was soon laughing so hard he couldn't read. By then we were all gasping for breath and wiping our eyes. We still laugh when we remember that night.

Emily Post wouldn't have approved of our table activities. For instance, the boys invented a game in which one would pick up an object—maybe the saltshaker—and jump it over the sugar bowl or the mashed potatoes while calling out a score. Each player made up the rules as he went along, scores sometimes depending upon the perceived merit of the food being jumped. We all found it hilarious. One night a visiting friend of Steve's tried to make sense of the game and of course failed. Not everyone liked the Smith brand of humor.

Basketball and baseball were important at our house. If Steve's team lost a game, he came to the table the next day looking despondent. We all knew that he blamed himself for every loss. Then the younger boys would step up their antics, hoping for a smile from Steve.

One morning Barney came to the table scowling. "I had an awful dream. Bad guys broke in, and I was the only one awake. They said they were going to kill us all, so I shot some of them and killed the rest with a knife." He glared at his father and me. "I saved all of us, and you punished me for playing with guns and knives."

We probably had our quota of family worries in the fifties, but I am thankful for the feeling of belonging at mealtimes.

In the uncharted days ahead I must cling to the America I knew, the one where I watched three boys grow up on a potato farm with willingness for hard work and time and space for play. I watched them learn from team sports to obey the rules and respect their opponents. It was my precious privilege to see my sons grow up safe and healthy, with the freedom to dream their dreams, make their choices, and speak their minds.

To survive now, I must hold to this, my America. I must believe that for future generations of kids, the freedoms will still be there.

# Part III

Often good luck rather than good management has improved my confused life. When my husband divorced me in 1973, when I was fifty-three, I ran into another problem I couldn't deal with: At that time no real estate dealer would show a desirable little house or apartment to a middle-aged single woman. When I'd asked about one apartment I liked, the agent told me he preferred to save it for a young couple. The only houses he showed me were such wrecks that I'd never have been able to repair them.

I was deciding that a mobile home was my best bet when my sister-in-law, Polly, asked if I wanted to buy the Hoyts' house. I had never seen the Hoyts' house, but I said, "Sure." That same day she asked the Hoyts if they would sell, and they said they would.

*Window-washing day at Glenna's house in Presque Isle, about 2005*

Almost instantly I had a house! That night Polly said I'd better go out and look at it before I signed anything. One look and I knew that the snug little house on its quiet dead-end street was the place for me, and I've been grateful for it for more than thirty-five years now.

Sometimes a friend asks why I don't take a vacation or go to Florida in the winter, and I tell her that if I didn't live in my house I'd be glad to rent it for myself for a week or a month, so why should I leave it? Besides, I like to be in Aroostook for all the rapidly changing seasons.

*Glenna poses for a photograph for* Echoes *Magazine in the late 1970s/early 1980s*

*Glenna's grandchildren and a niece frolic in a potato field in Aroostook County*

# The Street

NEARLY THIRTY-SIX years ago I bought a little house. Excited to own a home, yet worried about the responsibilities, I told myself I could sell the house if I couldn't manage. Still, I felt a chill of finality when I read the sign at the entrance to the street: DEAD END.

Even though I suspected I'd stay forever, and even though I added my paint and paper to the walls and my treasures and clutter to the shelves, I felt like an intruder. I started to feel at home only when I sat at the front window and watched the children—mostly girls at the time—playing in our half-street with no traffic.

I remembered my own childhood as I watched tiny ladies tottering up and down in their mothers' high heels. I saw dolls riding in carts and carriages, and little travelers pedaling by in plastic dragons and turtles.

The makeup of the child population has changed over the years. At present there are more boys than girls, yet one of my favorite days was an outdoor laundry project where everybody's doll clothes were washed in a blue plastic wading pool filled with soapy water, the washing action provided by many pairs of bare feet jumping up and down in the pool. Another wading pool full of clean water and more pairs of feet took care of the rinsing, and the little garments were hung on low lines strung from tree to tree on my neighbors' lawn. The wash came out to look remarkably clean, and at every stage of the process the boys worked along with the girls. No "women's work" on my street!

I feel at peace when on a summer evening I see a dad walking home with a tricycle in his hand and a sleepy boy on his shoulder. Toys, boots, and sweaters get dropped up and down the street through the day, but find their way home by bedtime.

In autumn, the old maples that line the street give us raking exercise as the leaves fall. We place the leaves in neat rows for the city truck to vacuum, but the truck is never quick enough to deprive the kids of dry leaves to run and bike through, pile up, and roll in. I like to scruff in them, too.

After a big snow last winter, I made many trips to the window to watch the construction of forts and tunnels, an older boy showing the little ones how to dig and build. I was disappointed when, on Monday, the city plow ruined the weekend's work.

Perhaps my favorite day on the street occurs in early April when the sun shines so hot that the snowbanks begin to look weak and ridiculous, and we defy them by rushing out without boots and mittens. Babies who don't remember last summer's sunshine bask in strollers while their mothers, sweaters unbuttoned, chat with neighbors along the way. Bikes, carts, and baseball gloves appear. One year on that special day, my next-door neighbors, a dignified young couple, started out for a walk. Very soon, though, she couldn't resist lagging behind and pelting him with a ball of wet snow, and he couldn't resist pushing her down in the snowbank where they laughed and rolled. At the first taste of spring we are all children.

And I will never forget an early-morning nude tricycle ride by a toddler who had momentarily eluded his parents. He pedaled furiously, all his baby fat jiggling. I hope I won't embarrass him by mentioning that ride.

I mark time by the milestones I view: the first wobbly bike ride without training wheels, Mom and Dad running along beside; the first day of school with its self-conscious parade of beginners looking scrubbed, brushed, and new, followed by parents with cameras. A few weeks later these pupils, now old hands at education, are running for the school bus while shouldering book bags big enough for college students.

Sometimes on the street there is a squabble, with tears and angry words. Soon, a mother appears and arbitrates, teaching the age-old lessons: be nice, take turns, play fair. Then my mind goes back nearly four decades to my little sons on the farm and the Dorsey kids from the next road. The seven of them held cat and dog circuses and revival meetings in the barn. They played baseball in the dooryard and Pullman tag at dusk when the shadows were scary. But occasionally one faction or another would come running into the house to tell me that never again would they speak to the other family. I would offer molasses cookies and milk before the final parting, and then they would go back to playing.

Sometimes I wish the leaders of the world and the nation would sit down and listen while their mothers tell them to behave themselves and stop being selfish. Then after they've had their cookies and milk they might see that one of their top priorities should be maintenance of a world where children can play.

I belong in my little house now, yet I watch the children more as years go by, and listen to their laughter—perhaps because I have more free time as I grow older. Or maybe it is because I have learned how soon little kids grow tall, walk quietly, and leave the street.

# My Life? The Cats' Meow

I WOKE UP ONE NIGHT thinking I heard a cat crying. It was a bitterly cold night, and I wondered if my cat Coty could have run out past me when I didn't see her. I rushed around the house until I found her sleeping in one of her soft places. Thinking I must have heard the wind howling, I went back to bed.

Later I woke up again to a cat cry so sad that I jumped out of bed again and looked out all my windows. Then by the glow of the streetlight I saw him in my driveway, huddled against the wind. I pulled on a jacket, went to my entryway door, and called to him. When he heard my voice he ran across the street to Mary's yard, looked at her door, and wailed again. Mary has no cats, so I knew he didn't live there. I called him again. "Mr. Gray Cat, I'll leave the door open and put a dish of food out."

Then I stood inside in the dark, watching. Slowly he came over, looking around every few steps. He came into the entry, saw the dry cat food, and gulped it down as if he hadn't eaten in days. When he finished, he jumped into a chair and curled up. Since he was only slightly warmer there than he would be outdoors, I opened the door slowly and spoke softly. "Do you want to come in where it's warm?" He stared at me and then ran away.

After that I put the food dish out every night and left the entry door partly open. Sometimes I'd see him eating. Usually the dish was empty in the morning. When Coty realized I was feeding another cat she would watch for him and try to drive him away. Then one day I saw a couple of neighborhood cats drop into the entry for a snack. Both are well fed at their home, but I guess everyone likes to eat out once in a while. I didn't mind having them there, but Coty, with growls and snarls, tried to make them leave.

I had asked my neighbors if they knew where Mr. Gray lived. They didn't know, but Mike told me Mr. Gray had attacked his cats and frightened them so much that they didn't dare go outdoors. "Oh, dear," I said, "and here I am feeding him." But Mike said that I should continue to give him food. By this time Mr. Gray would allow me to pat him, but he refused to come into the house.

Then one night my granddaughter Jasmine entered by the back door. "Is the kitchen door locked?" I asked.

"No," she said, "but there's a skunk eating cat food in the entry."

Although I wished the skunk no harm, my love of animals doesn't stretch far enough for me to adopt him. The next day I told Mr. Gray he'd have to come into the kitchen when he was hungry. I showed him where the dish was. After that, he would scratch to come in, but he'd leave as soon as he ate his dinner.

A few days later, I saw a woman walking across my lawn with a cat carrier. I asked if she had lost a cat. She told me she wanted to catch the stray gray cat and take him to the shelter. He had attacked one of her cats and torn its ear so much it had to be taken to the vet. She said the gray cat was a danger to the neighborhood cats because he probably had not been neutered or had his shots. I considered taking him to the vet, but since he looked like a purebred, and since he came by one day with a pregnant female who looked like him, I thought he might be somebody's breeding animal.

The little female ate in the entry that day, and then asked to come into the house. He followed her around as she sniffed into corners and looked everything over. Luckily for her, Coty was outdoors at the time. Finally she asked to go out and he followed. I never saw her again, but a few days after her visit Mr. Gray asked, for the first time, to come into the house for something besides food. He walked around and sniffed at all the places where she had gone, and then he stared at me. I assured him that I didn't know where she was. I've always wondered what happened to her.

Because I had learned to love this proud, dignified animal, I couldn't bear to have him lose his freedom. I told the woman with the carrier that I'd take him for shots and neutering. After that he traveled less, and neighbors said he no longer fought their cats. When winter came, my neighbor Steve made a bed for him in one of his work buildings, but the gray cat still came to my house for meals. I worried if he didn't come by for a few days.

*Mr. Gray, a stray who came to Glenna, cold and starving*

More and more I became aware of his noble nature. For instance, he got along well with neighbors Ed and Heather's kitten, Snowball. She would climb all over him when he was sleeping in the yard, but he didn't seem to mind. Then one day I heard Snowball crying loudly. I rushed to the door and saw that a yellow cat, a stranger to me, had cornered her by my door. Just as I started out to save her I saw Mr. Gray walking up the driveway in the slow-motion gait used by the cowboys in *The Wild Wild West* series. He stood between Snowball and Big Yellow. Yellow snarled and hissed; Mr. Gray just stared at him. Then Yellow took a step back, snarling and hissing again. Mr. Gray took another step toward him. They repeated this maneuver until finally Yellow ran off down the street. Mr. Gray nudged Snowball to make sure she wasn't hurt, and then he strode off in the direction taken by Yellow. I never saw Yellow again.

A couple of years ago Mr. Gray came to the door late one night, marched in, and looked for a soft place to sleep. I don't know why he decided to move in. He was getting older and slowing down; perhaps he sees my house as his retirement home where he is still free to come and go as he likes.

Mr. Gray continued to be noble in his treatment of Coty, who seemed to tolerate him outdoors, but who would growl and lash out at him in the house. He would find another place to sleep, but he didn't ever attack her. Then one night, after she kept following him around and growling, he finally went to the door and demanded to go out. He looked as if he had had all he could stand of her temper. A few hours later my next-door neighbor Marla telephoned to tell me that Mr. Gray was under her bed, and she couldn't get him out. I offered to go over and get him, but she said no, she liked him, and she didn't mind if he stayed, but she thought I might be worried. Marla's gray cat Smokey and Mr. Gray are friends, often visiting in the backyards or on my deck. I was heartbroken; he'd moved out to avoid Coty. I was relieved when he returned to my house the next forenoon. I quickly plied him with his favorite food.

Thus we three live together in what seems to be a dysfunctional family; I love both of them, yet they don't like each other. Coty likes to be in the same room with me, two old women together, but she has never been a lap cat. Mr. Gray likes to sleep in my lap. In his first months here he would run down cellar and hide if someone came to visit, but now he has decided that my relatives and friends will not hurt him. Sometimes he'll even jump on their laps.

Both cats see to it that I get plenty of exercise. Each goes out and comes in many times every day, and almost never at the same time. There are three doors in and out of my house; each will stand at a door and ask to go out, then saunter to another room and another door. Sometimes they ask to come in, and then when I reach the door they sit and think, and then change their minds. Each is fussy about food, liking something one week and refusing it the next. Mr. Gray often stays outdoors late at night in good weather, waking me up and asking to come in at two or three o'clock. Coty stays in at night but demands to go out at four or five in the morning.

Both have learned that I cannot put a sleeping cat out of a chair, so they can become instantly asleep in a chair I have vacated for long enough to get a cup of coffee. One day my son Mel gently put Coty out of a chair so he'd have a place to sit. She gave him such a look as Queen Victoria might have given to an underling who had pushed her off her throne.

No, life isn't perfect at our house. Yes, the cats are arrogant and spoiled. Yet I love to watch them strutting about, monarchs of all they survey. I love to watch them sleeping in their favorite sunny spots. I wouldn't have them any other way.

# Defense of "Old Woman"

I LIKE THE SOUND of the words "old woman." They're strong words—earthy, honest. I'm grateful I've survived long enough to be able to label myself by them. And yet, from many sources they've received a bad rap through the years.

The young coach says to his player, "You threw that ball like an old woman." The young husband admits to his wife, "I cried like an old woman at that movie." A businessman says to his partner, "Don't be an old woman. Take a risk." And when a young woman hears that her grandmother is going to marry an old friend, she says, "It's just for companionship, of course. They're old people. But honestly, sometimes they're so cute you'd almost think they're in love!"

And the commercials don't help. Good old women are fat and say "Mamma Mia!" as they stir the spaghetti sauce. And the less-than-admirable ones (by far the majority) are absent-minded and silly or petty and crabby. None of them know their way around the modern world; they learn about fast foods and laundry detergents from young-women-in-the-know.

And then there are the well-intentioned people who always put the adjective "poor" before "old woman." "Poor old woman, she rattles around all alone in that big house." It never occurs to them that she may be happily reading all the books and visiting all the friends she didn't have time for in her busy years. She's not necessarily sitting by the window like Red Riding Hood's grandmother, waiting for someone to bring her a cookie.

Some people consider the words "old woman" so insulting that they refuse to use them, substituting "elderly lady," which reminds me of furs, pearls, and lavender toilet water, or "senior citizen," which is a term too recently coined to be trustworthy. I prefer my "old woman" pictures of weather-beaten faces, gnarled knuckles, and ancient, faded, baggy-elbowed sweaters for going to the clothesline, the hen pen, the woodpile, and the berry patch.

Oh, I'll admit that in the 1920s most of the old women in my family felt they were all used up by the time they were forty-five. "I can't walk to the shore with you, dear—I'm an old woman," Great-Aunt Annie would say. But it wasn't old age that kept her from walking—it was probably all those days, after her daughter took over the heavy work, of sitting and mending and all those sugar-covered doughnuts and filled molasses cookies. We are able to take better care of ourselves today. We haven't had to ruin our health with our ancestors' backbreaking household drudgery and poor eating and exercise habits. We don't retire to the rocking chair, wrapped in a shawl, and weep over the baby shoes of our forty- or fifty-year-old children. Oh, I love my rocking chairs and my memories of my children growing up as much as they did. But life goes on, too precious to waste.

I know old women who do volunteer work in daycare centers, hospitals, homeless shelters, and libraries, and who play the piano for church. Old women take long walks, with time to see sunsets and sunrises. Some of us dig in the earth and raise things. Some of us see the world new through the eyes of a young grandchild. We may paint a picture, write a poem, sew a quilt, knit some mittens. Old women can be found on cross-country ski trails, on golf courses, at community swimming pools, and in weight rooms. After age sixty-five we take free college courses and high school night courses where we study all kinds of things: religion and philosophy, woodworking, drawing, conversational French, rug-hooking, and English literature. And through all these later days we retain the values, the experience, the self-control, the acceptance—and yes, the ability to love—learned from the traumas of youth and middle age.

I'll admit that being an old woman (or, I assume, an old man) requires a sense of humor and a quiet bravery in the face of worrisome aches and pains, in the need to tolerate wrinkles where firm, smooth skin used to be, in the acceptance of the decrease of strength and energy, the gradual loss of teeth, hair, hearing, eyesight, memory, and the ability to digest green apples. And yet I suspect that many of us can say hello to the mirror and admit that we live more comfortably with this less-than-perfect old face and body than we did with our teenaged or our twenty-year-old selves. Perhaps we can be more kind now to the person in the mirror and to others, too. Perhaps we no longer demand the impossible of our time and energy.

So come on, young whippersnappers! Listen to the words "old woman" (or "old man"). They don't sound so bad, do they? With a little luck and by the grace of God, you'll be one of us someday.

# Riding to Pat's House

BRENDA AND I start out on a sunny afternoon in late September. The car has been serviced, Brenda is driving, and I am happily gazing at fields, sky, and bright leaves. Twice before we have visited Pat's home on the coast, so we know the way. We have grapes and crackers and cheese for nibbling, and bottles of water. Life is good.

As we leave Houlton for Interstate 95, a light rain begins to fall, but it doesn't dampen my mood. However, by the time we get to Bucksport the fog is so thick that Brenda slows down so we can peer at the signs. We see a big collection of route numbers: 3, 15, 199, 175. Since we are not sure of the number we need, we pull over and unfurl the road map. We find exactly where Pat's house is, right on the bay. But the last little bit of road that takes us there doesn't have a number. Oh, well. We'll find it.

We drive for what seems a long time. Then Brenda says, "We're here! See? There's the historical society building that we visited last time we were here."

"But it's on the wrong side of the road," I say. "How do we get to Pat's house from here?"

"Don't know," Brenda says, "but we'll just drive until we find it."

We drive slowly on winding roads in rain and fog. Finally I read a sign. "We're entering Castine," I say.

"So we picked the wrong way," Brenda says. We turn around and go back.

"There's the historical society," I say. We drive on. The fog gets thicker. Finally I make out the words YOU ARE ENTERING BLUE HILL.

"Missed it again," Brenda says. "I wish I'd brought my cell phone." We drive on until we come to an unmarked road. "This must be it," she says.

"Oh, look!" I say. "There's the historical society again—or one just like it in a neighboring town."

We stop and study the map. Brenda points. "We haven't tried this route," she says. So off we go.

Finally I make out the words on another sign. "How do you feel about Stockton Springs?" I ask.

"Not good," Brenda says. "So we'll just go back to . . . wherever we were."

When the fog lifts a bit I say, "Look! There's the bay!"

"But it's on the wrong side. We're not supposed to be on this side of the bay. How did we get here? And how do we get back over on Pat's side?"

"Maybe there's a ferry," I ask. "You know, like the one on the River Styx in Hell?"

Brenda gives me a look.

"We'd better stop and ask," I say. "At a convenience store or a gas station or—"

"Have you seen one of those lately?" Brenda asks.

"Well, no. But there must be a post office, a town office, a bank—something."

"It's Sunday," Brenda says.

"Oh. Well, maybe we'll see someone out walking."

"In this rain?" she asks.

We keep driving. When the rain lets up a little we see two young men walking from a house to a pickup truck. Brenda drives into their yard, rolls down the window, and says, "We're lost. Can you help us?"

"Sure," the tallest one says. It turns out they know where Pat's brother Jim lives. We know that Pat's house is near Jim's. Saved at last.

The tall man points. "You go that way to the next intersection, then turn right where the road branches, bear left and . . . "

The other fellow interrupts. "There's a mess of construction there, remember? In this rain the road will be slippery. We'd better send them around the long way."

"Right," the tall one says. "You start out like I said, then take a sharp left at that bumpy place in the road—sort of like a little dip. You'll see what I mean when you get there. Then there's a blind corner, you take a sharp left, then straight ahead to Jim's house."

Just then the rain comes down in a torrent, and the two make a dash for their truck. "Thanks!" Brenda calls, rolling up the window.

"Did you get all that?" I ask.

"No," she says.

We have long since seen the last of the grapes and the crackers and cheese. We've consumed the last drop from our water bottles. I need coffee, food, a bathroom, and a security blanket. We drive on.

"Maybe we'll just happen to come to Pat's house," Brenda says.

"That last sign said something that looked like Moscow," I say.

"We're in Russia?" Brenda asks. We both laugh, and comment that China, Athens, and Norway aren't all that far away.

Then we see a sign that says NURSING HOME. The lights are on. Good! They don't close on Sunday. Brenda drives into the parking lot. Just as we get to the door a smiling woman comes up behind us, carrying a large tray with individually wrapped pieces of what looks like blueberry pie. We tell her our story. She doesn't know where Pat lives, but says we can borrow her cell phone. Brenda holds the pie tray while the woman reaches for her phone. Brenda says, "Tell me Pat's number." I rattle it off. "That's my number," she says. The only other number I can think of is mine.

"Just look at that pie," I say. Then the rain pelts down harder. The woman grabs her pie and her phone and rushes through the door, us right behind her. Brenda says we'll find the office and borrow a phone and a phone book.

When Brenda pauses to ask directions to the office, I glance into a cozy lounge room. One group is working on a huge jigsaw puzzle, others are playing checkers or watching TV. For a moment I wish I could stay here, especially since I suspect they'll have that pie for their supper.

We find an office with an attractive young woman at the desk. "We have a problem," Brenda says. Brenda looks stern and determined; I feel fretful and frazzled. The woman looks me over, and then says to Brenda, "Yes, I see. What's her room number?"

"No, no!" I proclaim. "I don't live here. I'm not staying."

Assuming that I'm deaf as well as old and crazy, the woman says to Brenda, "A lot of them say that. I'll call an attendant."

"Oh, no, she's not the problem," Brenda says. "We're lost."

The woman, new to the area, knows neither Pat nor Jim. But we find Pat's number in the book. Pat answers, saying, "I've been wondering where you were for an hour or so now."

"We've been right here in the neighborhood," Brenda tells her. Brenda listens to directions and seems to understand them. We start out again. I keep saying, "This doesn't look right," and Brenda says, "I know, but Pat said . . . "

We drive on. I say wistfully that maybe the next sign will say PRESQUE ISLE. Then miraculously, Pat's house! Or one like it in another town. But no—there's the real Pat on the deck, smiling and waving. I am always glad to see Pat and her house, but never so glad as at this moment.

I suspect that after this day Brenda won't travel far without her cell phone; I'm sure that never again will I traverse Maine without compass, a huge Thermos of coffee, sandwiches, cookies—and the phone numbers of everyone I know south of Bangor. And never on a Sunday.

# Morning Song

EVEN THOUGH I've lived through more than thirty-two thousand of them, each daybreak is delivered to me as an undeserved gift. There's the blast of cold air on my face when I go to the door for the paper, there's the first taste of red grapefruit, there's the joy of writing the first correct word in the new crossword puzzle.

The sun never comes up twice the same. Sometimes the tops of the fir trees in the backyard blaze orange against a dark sky. Sometimes blue tree shadows appear on a neighbor's house.

I watch splashes of color thrown on the ceiling and the walls by the prism hanging in the window. I see patterns on the floor from the sun shining through the sprawling fern. The sky behind the bare tree branches changes by the minute. I have to sit and stare so that I won't miss a red or a purple streak. I'm aware of the earth spinning as the sun hits one bookshelf and then another. Occasionally a book that I haven't opened for decades catches my eye as a sunbeam hits it. I may even walk over and take it from the shelf.

Usually the first voice I hear is the *prrrt* of my cat Coty telling me she wants to go out and play. The second voice may be the loud comment of a crow from the top of the tallest fir. Often he sits up there and taunts the cat.

This morning three large crows marched side by side up my driveway, pompous little men in black suits. Then two lagged behind, screaming at each other, jumping up and down and flapping their wings. The third strode on, ignoring them. Maybe that one was a woman in a black suit, bored with having men fight over her, or perhaps being coy. Soon she flew away and the gladiators followed. I'm glad I didn't fall back to sleep and miss that little drama.

For a while the street is empty of human activity. Then through my wicker screen in the window I see the fragmented flashes of Rick's red truck and Mary's red car, neighbors going to work. Later I see the bright yellow of a school bus. A pink jacket comes into view. Before going to work, Cindy is taking her little dog, Molly, for a walk. Knowing that neighbors are leading their routine lives tells me that all is well.

I hear a train whistle in the distance, and I imagine the backed-up traffic on Main Street as the line of boxcars goes clattering by, the names of faraway places readable in chipped paint on their sides. Since memory always dances with the present scene, I recall train rides in my childhood, rides to Ellsworth or Bangor or Waukeag or Tunk Lake stations.

I see Coty running across the yard, sun gleaming on her tiger stripes. She scratches at the door and I open it for her. I pat her soft cold fur and she purrs, but if I give one too many pats I'll be scratched. She finds a sunny spot on the floor and takes her bath.

On my way back from the door I pick a leaf from the dried mint plants hanging by the chimney. I rub it between my hands until it turns to nothing. The smell lingers. The telephone rings. My world is starting up for another day. I'll do some necessary chores—but not before I thank the universe for another morning.

# I Live Alone—I Think

IT IS TRUE THAT two others, Occupant and Resident, have used my mailbox for years; lately, however, there's another inhabitant. Nearly every week there's mail for Mr. Harold T. LaSalle. I hand it to the clerk, who after several weeks of this pattern, eyes me with suspicion.

"You're sure Mr. LaSalle doesn't live at this address?" she asks.

"It's a small house," I tell her. "I'd notice."

It's true that I'm old and absentminded; it's true that I lose things. But misplace something the size of Harold? Not likely. Unless he's a tiny sprite. But that's just silly. There's no such thing as elves and such. Still, if he were an elf my cats would catch him and bring him to me—dead or alive. I shiver at the thought. Surely Harold is of normal size. Unless he's a ghostly critter, wisping around here all the time; but invisible? If he's disembodied why does he receive catalogs for warm-up suits and running shoes? And why does he use my address? Maybe he's a criminal running from someone. Or maybe he's someone running from a criminal. But where could he hide? In my barn attic in the summer, maybe? Could he be in the cellar nesting behind the furnace in cold weather? If he's around, he must be eating fast food. I have missed neither food nor drink. That's not surprising, though. At this stage I'm not a very good cook, and I'm the only person in the world who likes my coffee.

One day the suspicious but helpful postal clerk says that maybe Harold T. LaSalle rented my post office box at an earlier time. I tell her I've had that box for more than forty years.

Surely Harold's associates could have caught on to a new address in all that time.

One day I see a strange man walking down my street. I decide he looks like a Harold. I rush up to him and say, "Hello, Harold!" He walks faster, muttering something like, "I'm not interested in you, old woman. Leave me alone." It was probably Harold, and he was afraid I'd blow his cover.

Then one day in my box there was a letter for Mr. Tom Fulton. Good heavens, I thought. Maybe Harold is pursuing Tom. Or maybe Tom and Harold are in cahoots. Tom got only that one letter, though, so I don't worry much about him.

Yet the mysteries never end. One day I go to the hospital to take some tests—I wasn't sure what for. I suspect they call in people my age and check our vital signs to try to figure out if we're still alive. Anyway, I give my health-care card to the receptionist and she asks me to take a chair in an empty waiting room.

A few minutes later she looks around the room and then at me. "Thurlow?" she asks. I stare at her. "Thurlow Atkins?" she asks, speaking louder.

"I'm Glenna Smith. Who's Thurlow Atkins?" I ask her.

"Why did you give me this card if you're not Thurlow Atkins?"

"Maybe someone gave me back the wrong card last time I was here," I say. "I never look at the name."

"That's possible," she says, but I could tell she didn't believe me. "Could you have picked up a wrong card where you live?"

"You think Thurlow lives at my house? No! Can't be. Unless he's hiding with Harold and Tom." She gasps, and rushes me off to my doctor's office. At least she's willing to admit that I'm not Thurlow, and a good thing, too, or I might have ended up with a prostate operation. At last they make me a new card. Then I think of poor Thurlow, with no hospital card. What if he needs an operation? I wonder if he has my card.

Things kept going downhill after that. One day when I answered the phone a pleasant-sounding woman said, "I'd like to speak to Galen, please."

"Galen who?" I ask.

"Galen Perry," she says.

"He's not here," I tell her.

"When will he be back?" she asks.

"That's hard to say," I explain. "I don't know Galen, you see, and—"

She raises her voice. "Look, I was given this number for Galen. I'm calling long distance and it's imperative I get in touch with him. Does he live there or doesn't he?"

I sigh. "Not unless he's visiting with Harold and them," I tell her.

"Then may I please speak to Harold?"

"Harold's not here."

"When will he be there?"

"Well, it's hard to say. I've never seen Harold, you see, but sometimes I think—"

"Thank you very much!" she yells, and she hangs up.

Honestly, some people.

That's the last that I've heard about Galen, but life isn't even close to being back to normal. Today a shiny green car drives into my yard. I scurry to the door, wondering who it can be. I'll make tea, and . . . a smiling young woman is knocking at the door.

"I've come to see Harriet," she says.

"Harriet who?" I ask.

"Harriet Ash. She gave me this address."

"Oh, dear," I say. "Is she a friend of Harold or Tom, or maybe Thurlow or Galen?"

She stares at me and backs away a step. "Harriet does live here, doesn't she?" she asks.

I throw my hands into the air. "Who can say for sure?" I wail.

# The Last Dinosaur

WHEN YOUNGER FRIENDS and relatives suggest that I buy a laptop, do e-mail, get online, buy a cell phone, and send text messages, I explain that I have a 1920s-model brain, which did not come equipped to deal with these contrivances. I ask if they would expect a 1920s Model T Ford to do everything a Ford can do today. Or would they expect from a treadle sewing machine the performance of today's magic stitchers? Well, then.

Truth is, I still love the Model T. If I were rich I'd buy one and keep it in the backyard for a pet. I'd sit in it, grasp the steering wheel, and make that bubbly noise with my lips that little kids make when they pretend-drive. In summer I'd fill the backseat with pots of geraniums. I love the treadle sewing machine, too. It was the last manufactured gadget that I could take apart, oil, and clean. I liked the soft *whirr* when I pedaled it; I liked being in complete control of speed and direction. I don't know the fate of Papa's 1925 Model T, but Mama's Singer sewing machine sits proudly in the home of a friend and serves as an end table.

My little brain was ten years old before it met a telephone. I remember the day when the cumbersome thing was attached to the wall of the Ashville Post Office where we lived. Unwieldy though it was, it still had a human side. If I put the heavy receiver to my ear and turned the crank—and I was usually the only one in my house who would do so—I would hear the voice of Eveline or Goldie, the operators in the little office at West Sullivan. Day or night, one of them was on duty and ready to report a fire or find the only doctor for miles around. When I rang, one would say,

"Hello, Glenna. What number do you want?" One village woman refused to use the thing, fearing the devilish substance that made it work might infect her brain and kill her. I trusted it because Papa always told me that science was wonderful.

Often my granddaughters bring cell phones to my house. Once Jasmine placed hers on the table, saying, "Answer it please, Gram, if it rings while I'm in the shower." I stood at a distance and eyed the tiny spaceship with its eerie blue lights. When it rang it played unworldly music. Gingerly I picked it up and pushed everything that looked movable. Nothing happened and I was glad. What if my old brain has no resistance to all this electronic hocus-pocus? I felt that if I kept away from that cell phone, maybe it wouldn't harm me. That avoidance philosophy got me safely through my eighties. Almost.

Son Mel and I were riding down Interstate 95, enjoying the sunshine and looking forward to a James Taylor concert, when he received a text message from his friend Marilyn, also traveling that day. Since Mel is a member of the last generation that doesn't find it necessary to do three other things while driving a car, and since he wasn't wearing his reading glasses, he handed the cell phone to me and asked me to read the message. Although the letters were tiny, I managed to decipher, "Where are you?"

"Answer it, Mum," Mel says.

I hold the thing at arm's length. "I don't know how to run it."

"It's just writing. See the numbers and letters at the bottom?"

I find them and by squinting I can read them. "What will I say?" I ask.

"Just say we're approaching Augusta, Mum. It's easy."

After poking a button several times, I find the w. I hunt, but I can't see how to make it a capital letter. I give up, and make an e, which I add to the w. Then I need a space. I try a few things, and finally get a whole row of punctuation marks. I'm glad to know they are there, for soon I'll need a period. That's if I ever manage to make a whole sentence. But spaces? I ask Mel, who is grinning at my ineptness. Now I write a space and then *are*. There. I have two whole words, *we are*. Oops! I tell Mel that I think I accidentally hit SEND.

"What did it say?" he asks.

"We are," I say. He laughs.

"Actually, that's profound," I tell him. "We exist. Surely she will figure out that if we exist we are still moseying along toward Portland."

"Try again," he says.

When Mel turns into the left lane to allow a car to enter from a ramp, I can't see the screen in the glare of the sun. I lose *we are*. I get it back, though. Maybe I'll get the hang of this after all. Then I hit wrong keys again—my fingers are 1920s models, too—and put too many g's in *Augusta*.

"Drat it," I say, "I misspelled Augusta. I'll have to do it over."

"Don't bother, Mum," Mel says. "We left Augusta a few minutes ago. Now we're nearing Auburn and Lewiston." He still thinks this is funny.

"I'll settle for Auburn," I say. "Fewer letters."

Mel mentions that his daughter Hillary text-messages so fast that she scarcely looks at the screen.

"Good for her," I mutter. "Oh, dear, I lost it again. I'll start over. Now where is that *a?*"

"Forget Auburn," Mel says. "We'll be in Portland in a few minutes. I'll call her then."

At this point Mel is laughing so hard that he is gasping for breath. I had to laugh, too. At least he now understands the limits of my abilities. I hope I never try text-messaging again, but I've learned never to say never—no sense to tempt the fates. I'll just try to be happy with what my vintage brain can manage. I can't go back to Eveline and the human telephone, though. Actually, I wouldn't mind trying bonfires and smoke signals.

# The Telephone Man

WHEN MY TELEPHONE rings and a strange voice assures me that if I change something—perhaps an insurance company or a service—I will save heaps of money, my stock answer is: I like things as they are. I'm too old to make big changes. When I've made changes in the past, I always ended up paying more.

However, last week a woman with a great voice—she sounded like a real human being—talked me into changing my telephone company. True, I am dissatisfied with some of my phone service, but it was her voice that won me over. When she said that I must be at home the following Tuesday from noon until two, I readily agreed. She said that if the installer didn't arrive until after two o'clock, my service charge would be waived.

As soon as I thought about it, I regretted my hasty choice. Although I keep my house at a level where I can be happy every day, I don't meet anybody's standards for good housekeeping. The big problem is that my house is small, I've lived in it for thirty-six years, and I seldom throw anything away. The place is so full of stuff that I get nervous when a service person tries to get around and fix something.

On Tuesday the telephone man's big truck arrives at exactly twelve. I go to the door and say, "This is the right house."

"I know," he says, striding around to the outside wall where electricity enters.

He stays out there for several minutes. Good, I think. Perhaps he doesn't have to come into the house at all. Then I see him dragging a long, heavy wire across the street. He puts up his tall ladder and pulls the wire up to a pole. Then he notices that the wire is caught on a branch of my partially dead maple tree. He keeps trying to flip the wire above the branch, with no luck. Finally I go to the door and tell him he can cut the branch off if he needs to. The poor old tree loses branches when the wind blows hard, so one more won't matter. He walks to the tree, jumps up, and grabs the branch. It breaks off. He goes back to his ladder and continues to work.

A while later he comes to the door. I hope he will tell me that I'm all set with my phone, but he asks the way to the cellar. I point to the door and tell him where the lights are. Then I wonder what he'll find down there. I'm glad I cleaned up the litter box this morning. All kinds of things are stored in boxes on shelves, but he does have room to move around. I'm just glad he doesn't have to come into the house.

Oh, no! Later he comes upstairs and starts across my tiny living room. He's headed for the corner where I nest for a few hours every day, reading the *Bangor Daily News*, doing word puzzles, writing letters, crocheting, reading a book. When I sit I am surrounded by a hamper full of yarn, a basket with whatever I'm crocheting, stacks of magazines I've been meaning to give away, bookcases full of books, family pictures, pencils, pens, and several quart jars full of buttons—I've never discarded anything without cutting the buttons off first. Mama and Grammie always said you never know when you'll need a certain button. I haven't needed a button from the jars in years, but there they sit, at the ready. Then there are boxes of books. I keep giving books away, but also I keep buying them. There are boxes of loose papers waiting to be sorted. And cartons of greeting cards sent by family and friends. How can I discard such beautiful things from such dear people? And there are all my houseplants, which I have allowed to run wild. Sometimes they reach out and grab people.

I can thread my way to my chair, but the telephone man is tall, and his feet are longer than mine. Where will he step? I hurry—well, not really. My hurrying is slow these days, but I start moving piles of stuff from the corner onto the sofa, the chairs, and the coffee table. Meanwhile, he has removed a large jar of knitting needles and crochet hooks from the TV shelf; also, a picture of my great-granddaughter and several candles. He doesn't know what to do with them. I add them to the piles on the sofa and hope a cat won't jump up and push the whole stack to the floor.

Now he is trying to pull the heavy TV out from the shelf. Oh, dear—when was the last time the space back there was cleaned? My grandson-in-law did a great job on all those shelves—was it last year or earlier? The telephone man is trying to see behind the TV. I am trying to move the heavy chair, to give him a place to put his feet. I try to move a stand and a hamper out of the way. Alas, in my house there is no out-of-the-way. I should take them outdoors since the sun is shining. At least I've cleared standing space for him. I sit down on a stack of magazines on the sofa, pick up a cookbook from the stack beside me, and start to read. I'm trying to quiet my nerves.

Surely he must be nearly finished. But no, he's heading for the door. He needs to get a tool from his truck, he says. And I have filled in his path. He takes a tentative step and there is a sickening crunch. I see that it is nothing, really, just a toy that neither cat plays with anymore. But the telephone man jerks back and his foot lands on some glossy magazine. He starts to skid, to lose his balance. Oh, please don't fall down, I whisper. In my house there is no free-falling space. If you fall you crack into the hard edge of something or other. He is so tall he looks like a giant Gulliver about to topple in the land of the Lilliputians. I can envision his head hitting the corner of a table. I see blood spurting. I hear the ominous wails of the ambulance. The telephone company will sue me for unsafe working conditions. I may go to prison for my last years. At least there'll be no clutter in my cell.

At last he catches his balance and with a few more false starts—I'm trying to run ahead of him and push stuff in all directions—finally he makes it to the door and on to his truck. I wait to hear the truck start, feeling that he will now make a clean getaway. He remains in the truck for some time, but he doesn't run away. He may be hyperventilating. He may be so frustrated with me that he can't force himself back inside. I admire him for being so businesslike, so intent on doing his job. Surely he won't hit an old woman who gets in his way at every turn?

Finally he comes back with a black box and asks for the location of the nearest outlet. "Right there beside the TV shelf," I say. "But it hasn't worked in ages. I've been meaning to call the electrician and—" He just stares at me. I point to another outlet on a more-distant wall. Then I realize that, since I had no idea he'd go there, I've completely filled that path. I'm panting now, but I gather up stuff and try to stack it on the already-loaded sofa.

The telephone man looks around and sighs. Then he asks if the bookcases are fastened to the walls. I tell him I think so, that my son built them solid at the time. He points to a shelf, asks if he can bore a hole there. I nod. I won't even tell you how he goes to the truck again to get the most massive boring equipment I've seen. Where will he stand to wield that long bit? I can't even think of anything I can move to help him. I've done myself out of a place to sit and my old legs are giving out. I lean on the chimney and take in the chaos. It looks as if the entire NCIS squad had turned everything upside down in search of evidence. I feel an attack of insane laughter coming on. I manage to stifle it. I am quite sure that the telephone man sees no humor in the situation.

He stops drilling and then struggles to thread a cord through and around and over stuff to get to the outlet. Success! He plugs in the black box. Surely he is finished? Then he asks if there is another phone in the house. "Yes, upstairs," I say. "It's a little car, and when it rings you hear a car horn. One of my sons gave it to me a long time ago. One of the wheels has fallen off, so you have to put it down just right or it disconnects. It's on the far wall by the window, sitting on a tray with pictures of cars on it. The tray is on a trunk."

The poor man just stares at me again. As he climbs the stairs I wonder if there's a path between the encyclopedias I left on the floor yesterday, all the plastic storage containers, and more boxes of books. But he's on his own. Both my cats are up there sleeping, and if Coty is annoyed at being awakened she may attack him with tooth and claw—another reason why I'll be sued. Oh, well, I've had a good life. Finally he comes back downstairs, and there are no visible bleeding wounds. He thrusts a manual into my hands, mutters that both phones are working, and bolts for the door.

I wonder if he will rush off and quit his job. Oh, I hope not. I hope his next job is in a huge neat house with handy outlets, no dead branches to catch on wires, no impediments at all. Perhaps he'll be late getting there because he has been here so long. Then some lucky devil won't have to pay his installation fee.

# The Crows of March

AT DAYBREAK on a March morning last year I was awakened by the strident voices of two crows—one sitting on the topmost twig of the tallest spruce in the neighborhood, the other perched at the top of the next tallest tree, an oak. The two shrieked at each other in voices so venomous that they must even have been an embarrassment to other crows, themselves no Dean Martins.

Since it's way warm for March I bundled up and took my coffee to the deck where I could eavesdrop. Although I can't understand all of crow talk, I got the gist. The spruce tree visitor yelled, "Hark! Hark! I'm on top of the Earth! Earth!"

"False! False! False!" screamed the other. "Half-dead old spruce. Soon your branch will Crack! Crack! Crack!"

"Rascal! Knave! Why? Why? Why?"

" 'Cause! 'Cause! 'Cause!"

When they tired of taunting each other they branched out to all the ills of their world. Then I realized that the oak tree crow was a Republican and the spruce tree inhabitant, a Democrat. From the oak Republican I learned that the abominable weather ("Too hot for March! March! March!") and the sorry state of the Corn! Corn! supply were the Fault! Fault! of nobody but the head crow. From the spruce Democrat I learned that certain birds, declaring that they would Seek! Seek! for nothing but the truth about the corn situation, devoted their lives to the Wrack! And Ruin! of the head crow.

Finally I called out to them, "If you can't say something nice, why don't you both keep quiet?"

Then the one nearest me squawked, "Who is the oversized old bird who Cawed? Cawed?" Then he glided off his perch and swooped so low that I covered my head for fear of what might fall on it. He'd be just mean enough. The two returned morning after morning, always loudly snarling.

This year on a March morning I wasn't surprised to be awakened by crow voices. I looked out expecting to see last year's duo, but these birds were different. I counted eleven in the big oak, chatting in groups of two or three, sounding animated but not angry. I watched and listened. Finally I noticed that all the groups were watching two crows who were by themselves on a far branch. They seemed to be cooing—or as close to cooing as a crow can get. They ruffled their feathers and joined their beaks. As their ardor became more intense and as they realized they had an audience, one cackled, "Your hackmatack or mine?" and they flew away, discussing in which section of the piney woods they'd like to raise their kids.

Once the happy couple had departed, there was that sad, silent moment that occurs at weddings after the last drinking of toasts and the last throwing of rice—after the bride and groom drive off into their new lives. Silently the other crows glided away.

Why were these crows so different from last year's? Were they a different breed? I never can tell crows from ravens. Or had they changed? Perhaps they had learned that they feel better if they don't screech at each other, and that they feel cleaner if they don't scratch around in the political mire. Or they may simply have decided that it's better to make love, not war.

# Single and Invisible

A DIVERSITY OF COUPLES live there in harmony. Black, white, beige, yellow, old, young, high, low— my top drawer is a melting pot of sock togetherness.

The oldest, a soft lavender pair, belonged to one of my granddaughters when she was in a grade-school, purple-loving stage. However, when she was a college freshman and living with me, having moved on with her tastes, she discarded the lavender socks. When I found them in her wastebasket I saved them. All these years I've loved them, so soft and warm inside my sneakers. But even the best of relationships may come upon hard times.

One morning when I paw around in the drawer for my old friends, I find only one.

No! How can they separate after such a long and happy time together? I look again. No luck. Who's to blame? Sometimes I suspect the washer and dryer of trickery. "She's getting too self-satisfied," they say. "We'll chew up a sock or two." Or one of the cats could be the culprit. They use rolled-up socks for hockey pucks and eventually lose them in a dark hole after pushing them down the cellar stairs, or they send the socks under the old divan where things live for months.

Did I set it aside because it needed darning? No. In all these years neither sock had ever had a hole. (Is my generation the last to darn socks? Probably. Yet, I couldn't escape the ghostly glares of my women forebears if I didn't save socks as long as possible.) I look under the washing machine rotator, a shady hideaway for straying socks. I retrace the trail from the dryer through the dimly lit cellar where sometimes a sock falls by the wayside. One sunny day I hung clothes on the line. I must go to the backyard and look around in case a delinquent sock jumped from the basket and hid in the grass. My whole day is in danger of going down the drain.

At last, admitting defeat, I thrust the abandoned sock into the pile at the back of the drawer with all the others who have lost mates and who lurk there in purgatory. Ever the optimist, I let these loners pile up there for months—years sometimes. I fear that if I throw one away I'll find the other in a day or so, hiding in a boot or resting in a bag of stuff tossed into the barn attic, waiting to be sorted later. Sometimes a sock just comes back on its own, returning perhaps because it misses its mate.

At last one day when I yearn for warm socks I do a daring thing: I wear old lonesome lavender with another single—a black sock with brown owls on it. How I had loved wearing those owl socks with my sandals and looking down at the wise old birds. My feet feel cozy in my mismatched mates as long as I don't look down at them.

But emotions in the sock drawer run amok. "A mixed marriage!" "What can she see in him?" "Owls and lavender don't belong together—it says so in the Footwear Bible." "This will be the end of society as we know it." "Why couldn't they just stay sad, single, and out of sight?"

Sorry to have caused such a stir, I don't appear with that pair again. In fact, I resort to buying a dozen pairs of identical socks while muttering to the universe, "You can't trick me now!" But I find enforced conformity constricting, diversity exciting. I just can't help it.

I have learned to be oh so careful when loading the washer. I make sure the socks are all in there two by two, like little buddies at the swimming pool, teenagers at the prom, retired couples on a cruise, animals on the ark.

Yet the population of purgatory grows. How does this happen? I guess I must accept that I didn't come into the world equipped with answer books.

Oh, dear! Where is the other orange sock with the daisies? I remember the old song, "Where Have All the Flowers Gone?" Is the answer, my friends, blowing in the wind on the clothesline?

# Snowed In

THE SNOW CAME DOWN hard last night. This morning son Mel calls and asks if I plan to leave the house today. When I tell him no, he says he will wait until the storm is over before he plows me out.

There's a holiday feeling about being snowed in—an I'll-do-whatever-I-like feeling. I'll think of something really great. But first there's my morning routine of pills, exercise (strenuous for me but not much compared to what younger people can do), breakfast, and the word puzzles in the *Bangor Daily News*. And then I'll think of something.

But since this is Friday I must put the garbage out, to be picked up at about eleven. I empty the wastebaskets and check the refrigerator. I might as well throw out last week's casserole. Or was it the week before's? The snow is so deep that I need my high boots for going to the garage for a big plastic container. For years I just put the garbage bags out by the street, but then the hungry crows started shredding the bags and strewing remnants of my private life all over the place. I love crows, but there is stuff I'd just as soon my neighbors don't see.

I look in my downstairs closet. Finally I find one boot. Lord only knows where the other one is. I don't think I wore these boots at all last year. I tug at boxes and bags until the den floor is piled with them. Here's my boot! It was under a box of old handbags I've been planning to throw out. I'll put them out now, with the garbage. Oh, here's the L.L. Bean bag that I loved. Since it's washable I might as well keep it a while longer. And this patchwork bag. There's a little tear, but I could easily mend it. Maybe that will be today's project—cleaning out this closet since all the stuff is hauled out anyway.

But I'm all out of breath. I'll just sit for a few minutes and drink my coffee. I'll check to see what's on TV while I'm sitting here. Here's an old Ava Gardner–Clark Gable movie on Turner Classics. I saw it years ago but I can't remember much about it. I remember that Clark Gable passed through Presque Isle during the war. He stayed at a hotel for the night and somebody I knew saw him shove a woman aside so he could use the telephone in the lobby. Anyway, I still think he's a hero. I'll watch for a minute while I finish my coffee. I fall asleep in my chair. Oops! I wake up at ten-forty. Must hurry and get the garbage out. I pull on the books and take my cane. I get dizzy when it's all white out. It feels good, being out in the cold air.

I'm out of breath when I get back in and get the boots off. I'll sit down a minute and see if I can finish the crossword puzzle. Most every evening my friend Pat and I have a phone visit, and if she says the puzzle was easy and I still have blank squares in mine, well, I feel just awful. The house feels so warm and cozy after being out in the cold that I fall asleep again.

I wake up to see two cats sitting and staring at me. It is snowing so hard that they don't want to go outside, yet they hate to use the litter box in the cellar. They blame me for the weather. They try all three doors, find it's storming outside every one of them, then chase each other up and down the stairs, howling and snarling. I always thought that when I got old I'd have gentle, loving cats. Mr. Gray usually has a good disposition, though. He likes to sit in my lap when I watch ball games. He stares at the game. Coty, never a lap cat, sleeps in the chair beside us. Sometimes after the game I stare at something that doesn't interest me just because I don't want to disturb the cats. After all, they're old and set in their ways, like me.

The telephone rings and I'm glad to hear the voice of my granddaughter Jasmine. But I can barely hear her. My left ear has shut down, and that's my good ear. I'll go get the eardrops. I'm glad that most of my parts still work, after a fashion and with lots of help. I've had to give up long walks and instead walk in stores, pushing a cart for balance. But I'm grateful for the things I can do. I always loved to dance, partly because I liked snuggling up to some lad I had a crush on. But I've learned that dancing is fun for its own sake. That's one thing I can do for fun today—play some peppy music and dance. My only partner would be a chair back in case I get dizzy. I don't move fast, but I still like moving to music.

But I'll take another crack at that puzzle before I dance. Where's my pen? I buy cheap pens by the dozen, and yet there is never one in the room I'm in. Must be one here somewhere. Oh, here are the family pictures from last summer. I wondered where they were. That's what I can do today, put them in an album. But first I must organize some albums so each will contain Ashville pictures or farm years pictures or . . . I'll just sit here and look at the pictures for a few minutes and remember what a great time we had.

I might as well have some lunch before I start work. Some leftover corn chowder and a bran muffin would be good. I always doze off after lunch for a few minutes, so I check Turner Classics again. Ah, an old musical with Fred Astaire and Ginger Rogers. I like to doze to music. I hope my left ear comes back before the telephone rings again.

Now I'm wide awake and ready to work. I wonder why it's getting so dark. Four o'clock? Can't be. That's when I prepare my supper so it will be digested by bedtime. I sure do like storm days; the snow is still peacefully falling. I'd better put those bags and boxes back in the closet or I'll trip over them in the night. I can organize those pictures after supper. Or maybe there's a

Celtics game. Anyway, I'll get up earlier than usual tomorrow and get right to work.

I always get a lot done on storm days.

# I Learned It Somewhere

ON MY EIGHTY-FIFTH birthday I awoke to the first shards of light and asked myself, "What have you learned in all these decades that's of any use to you now?"

First I thought that I have to keep my soul—or whatever you call it—in good condition by keeping in touch with something universal. Then I've learned that, to keep my body working as well as possible, I must eat right and exercise.

Next I thought about my hardworking and long-abused feet. I often crammed them into ridiculous footwear: maroon suede pumps with three-inch heels; platform sandals that, had I fallen from them, would have caused broken bones; moccasins worn over bare feet; green alligator pumps with sassy French heels and pointy toes—that pair I loved so much that I still have them and I may fill them with cement one day and use them for bookends. The most sensible things I wore were ninety-nine-cent sneakers. At last I have learned to wear sneakers most of the time, keeping a clean pair for dress-up. True, today's sneakers are, even on sale, fifty times more expensive than their ancestors, the Keds. They are now called walking shoes for those of us who can no longer run, and they are so scientifically designed that I suspect they will keep me walking several weeks after I die. Inside these marvels I pamper my feet with the softest, spongiest white socks I can find.

I've learned that change happens, and that it's a waste of time to brood about what used to be and what I could once do. To paraphrase Goldie Hawn, "Today I'm the youngest I will ever be, and I had better make the most of it."

I've learned to accept myself—sometimes even to like myself. In earlier decades I often felt guilty that I wasn't a better mother, better wife, better schoolteacher, better housekeeper. Always I wanted to be thinner, smarter, and more organized. Now every morning I smile at myself in the mirror and say, "Congratulations, old thing! You made it through another night!" Then I thank all the gods and goddesses of the universe for the gift of another day.

I've learned to love the space around me. Once on a radio call-in show, a Mars Hill woman told Dewey Dewitt that she lived in the most beautiful spot in the world. Dewey asked if she had lived in many places. "Lived right here all my life," she said. I'm with her. I have learned that Maine, especially Aroostook, especially Presque Isle, especially my little street and my little house, is exactly where I want to be.

Although my little house is crammed with books, family pictures, plants—a lifetime of stuff—I've learned that things are not as valuable as ideas. Imagination is important. When I am stuffed into an MRI machine I ward off claustrophobia by floating down a little stream in a canoe. If I wake up in the night and can't get back to sleep I make up wild stories. I am the heroine in most of them. Despite the teacher who assured me that I was ordinary and without talent, I've learned to trust myself and dare to enjoy making up a poem or a play. I learn from my failures.

It is necessary for me to have a passion for something. For years, working with high school plays filled my mind and many of my hours, and made me happy. Always reading has been a part of me. Now, since cataract surgery, the ability to read seems more precious than ever.

Time, which for years pulled and prodded me through my days, has now become my friend. I wear a Mickey Mouse watch. I feel that if I measure my days by the dictates of a rodent in red pants, time can't be all that important. If I want to stare for an hour at the wind blowing the trees, I do.

At last I've learned to be aware of the world around me. I use all my senses all the time. I watch sunsets and Red Sox games. I hear the music of kids laughing and rain falling. I smell coffee and lilacs. I taste oranges and chocolate. I've learned to eat slowly and savor every bite. I feel my cats' fur, warm in the sunshine; I feel old soft towels and sheets.

I've learned to appreciate modes of travel. Once I loved running through fields of clover, daisies, and buttercups. I loved horse carts, merry-go-rounds, and Papa's Model T. I have loved riding in boats, trains, and planes. My greatest luxuries: two sports cars—a Saab Sonett when I was fifty, divorced, and feeling worthless, and at seventy, a Mazda RX-7 just so I wouldn't feel old. I drove them fast on I-95. I think a guardian angel watched over me. (Occasionally a state trooper got into the act also.) Now I love my ancient Neon. When I go to my old farm to visit my son, Mel, early on a Sunday morning, I drive below the speed limit and enjoy the fields and farms.

The older I grow, the more I learn that people are more important than anything. Good neighbors make me feel safe. Good friends add joy to my days and love me, despite my failings. I like saying hello to former students when we meet on the post office steps. And most of all, I've learned the value of family. My parents and grandparents and all the ones before them, they are all a part of me. I see some of them in my face, I hear them in my voice. I will always be a part of my sons and granddaughters. That may be a scary thought to the girls; I keep pointing out to them that they have inherited all my bad habits, absentmindedness and daydreaming among others. Like it or not, we're all stuck together. On my porch I have a sign: FAMILIES ARE FOREVER.

I can't define love, but I know it when I see it, and I've learned its power. All kinds of love make us human—love of parents and children, love of home and country, love of friends, neighbors, pets, nature. And then there's the wonderful love of the special person whose presence makes the eyes shine and the heart beat faster, the love that binds two together and makes them both better people than either could be alone.

There. That's all I've learned that amounts to much. Maybe in the days I have left, I'll learn more.

# Fiction

Sometimes I have a hazy memory of a person or event but I can't recall enough details to write an essay. Then I rely on my imagination and write what might have happened.

My fiction is true to a real idea even though the specifics are of my making. Or perhaps I think I know the truth but have no proof, since all the people in the story are long gone. Then I change some names and places and call it fiction. Usually I get more positive feedback from my stories than I do from my essays. Perhaps a spoonful of make-believe makes truth more palatable?

# My Brother Victor

WHEN I RETIRED after thirty years as post-mistress here in Northridge, I determined to spend a summer living the dream of my lifetime. I'd rent a cabin by a lake—a cabin with a little porch and a rocking chair.

Way up at Clarkson's Pond I found the perfect place, and since it was too tiny for a family, I could afford it. When I went to the real estate agent's to pay, I felt eighteen instead of seventy-eight.

"Do you have a husband?" the agent asked.

"No."

"Well, I'm afraid I can't rent the cottage to an old woman alone—a senior citizen. Too many break-ins—not safe."

*Oh no!* I thought. Then I heard myself say, "Oh, I won't be alone. My brother will be with me."

That statement would have shocked my parents—they lived and died thinking I was an only child.

"What's your brother's name?" the agent asked.

I glanced at the open *Bangor Daily News* on his desk: RED SOX THE VICTORS.

"Victor," I said. "Victor J. Baldwin."

"How old is he? How is his health?"

"He's fifteen years younger than I am. Big strapping man. Outdoorsman."

I thought of the old rhyme: "Whispering's lying, lying's sin—when you get to heaven they won't let you in." I realized that with every lie that escaped my lips, the gates of heaven were creaking shut.

"Outdoorsman! Good!" the agent said, "We'll sign him up for the horseshoe tournament."

"Oh! I'm afraid not. Victor's stone deaf, you see. Accident. Years ago, but he gets embarrassed when he can't understand people."

"Too bad. But we'll find something for Victor."

"Very kind. But he likes being alone. Reads a lot."

By now I knew the pearly gates had clanged shut forever, and I was only beginning to lie.

In the month before moving to the camp I had address labels printed for Victor. He ordered catalogs, newspapers, and magazines. All summer he got more mail than I did.

Then I drove to the coast, hundreds of miles from Northridge. Yard sales yielded for seventy-five cents a big black-and-red-checked jacket to hang on the porch. For a dollar I found a huge pair of old L.L. Bean hiking boots to put by the door. And my luckiest find of all—an inflatable man. I'd seen one advertised: "A woman can drive safely with a man in the car." This one had never been taken from the package, so I had to pay a dollar and a half for him. I blew him up and was pleased that he neither cracked nor leaked. I dressed him in yard-sale loot. I even bought him a red baseball cap since he was named for the Red Sox—sort of.

His clothes looked good on him, but his rubber face showed. So I found a gray wig and cut it up for a scraggly mustache and beard. Scruffy strands of hair showed under the baseball cap. With poster paints I wrinkled and weathered the bit of his face that still showed. He looked rough but real—if you didn't get too close.

At the cabin I refined my deceptions. While I was downstate I'd bought a pipe and tobacco. I'd light up and blow smoke on Victor and on his clothes on the porch.

June and July passed happily for Victor, my cat Velvet, and me—yet I marvel, looking back, that my trickery wasn't exposed. One over-curious person could have ruined everything. Still, I've always believed that if we old women are quiet and clean and neat and mind our own business, we are often invisible. The Clarkson area was busy with boys' and girls' camps, hikers, and tourists. Victor and I didn't create much of a stir.

I took him for a ride every evening so people were aware of him. I picked up a stack of mysteries for him at the library each week—I also took home the gentle romances the librarian assured me women of my age just love. I intended to return the romances unread, but I devoured them along with Victor's books.

"I wish Victor would come in someday," Elsie Pierson, the librarian, said. I explained his unease with strangers and she understood, and she continued to save the very best British mysteries for him.

I grew bold. Sometimes Victor reclined on the side porch with just a bit of him showing from the path. He often slept with a newspaper over his face. When I did errands he napped on the couch. I locked the doors, so if anyone looked through the window they'd see the back of a big man under an afghan. Usually Velvet slept beside him. Velvet liked a quiet man who didn't pester her.

I grew smug with success. I decided I'd write a book someday: *Every Single Lady Needs a Rubber Brother.*

Often Victor was an advantage. Explaining that he didn't like to be left alone for long, I avoided campers' meetings, costume nights, and talent contests. I even began to make plans for the fall. Perhaps Victor and I would buy a small secondhand camper and tour the country.

Then during my last week at Clarkson's Pond, the sheriff telephoned. "Awful sorry to bother you, Miss Baldwin, but there's been a break-in and someone stole a TV set. The only clue is footprints made by big L.L. Bean boots. Somebody remembered Victor's boots and somebody else said maybe him being such a recluse and all, he might not be just right in the head. I'm afraid I'll have to come out and look around."

I thought fast.

"Oh, Sheriff Adams, I was just going to call you. Victor's wandered off. I'm afraid he's had a spell. I've hunted for an hour. I'd appreciate some help, hunting . . . "

"Well now, I'll be right along soon as I give the kids from the boys' camp a tour of the jail."

I prayed those kids would ask a lot of questions. And I worked fast.

First I poked a hole in Victor, deflated him, and stuffed him, clothes and all, into a large garbage bag. What to do with him? No time to dig a hole. I locked the bag in the trunk of my car and put garbage in on top of him. Then I went to Victor's room and blew smoke around and pushed some magazines onto the floor. Victor never was a neat man. Then I opened the bureau drawers. What if the sheriff realized that Victor owned neither underwear nor pajamas?

The sheriff arrived with a young deputy and a hound, none of whom looked particularly interested. The dog sniffed the jacket and ambled across the rocks to the pond, where he took a long drink.

"Just as I feared," the sheriff said. "Your brother walked in the edge of the water. Prince can't pick up the scent."

*Good for you, Victor,* I said to myself. I hated to think of Victor out there wandering around lost, but that was better than admitting he was dead in a garbage bag.

On and off for the next couple of days, campers volunteered to search along with the deputies. A guilty conscience prompted me to make mounds of sandwiches and cookies and gallons of coffee and lemonade for the searchers.

The sheriff said I was a wonderful woman. So caring and brave.

Public opinion about Victor was divided. One hiker had observed, when he walked by the cabin, an evil look in Victor's eye. He wouldn't be surprised if Victor had murdered somebody.

The librarian was furious that people were maligning that wonderful man who read all those books—she'd seen a twinkle in his eye when we drove by one day. Why, he even waved to her.

Everybody talked about Victor. I heard a woman say loudly to the librarian, "I'll bet he's not her brother at all. I'll bet he's her boyfriend. Probably he's married."

"He's her brother," Elsie said. "Why, they look just alike."

*Oh my*, I thought.

The next day the stolen TV was recovered when thirteen-year-old Kevin Anderson tried to pawn it. A search of the Anderson house revealed Victor's boots. I had thought I'd absentmindedly put them somewhere. Kevin finally admitted he'd seen the boots when he stopped to ask me for a donation for the boys' club, and he had hatched his scheme.

"Did you do something to Victor?" the sheriff asked.

"No!" Kevin said. "I wouldn't hurt Victor. He's a nice man."

"He's lying," the sheriff said to me.

"I think he's telling the absolute truth," I said.

Finally, Kevin was released into the custody of his parents, and Victor's good name was restored. But still he hasn't been found.

"Some fall, a hunter will find his bones," the sheriff said.

Back in Northridge people had read the papers, and I had to answer questions about the brother nobody had heard of. I explained that he was a half-brother who had run away from home when he was fifteen. "But when he was a little tyke," I said, with a catch in my voice, "I was like a second mother to him."

A week later I had a quiet private ceremony for saying good-bye. Velvet watched while I incinerated Victor in the oil drum in the backyard. I really did miss him. I said to Velvet, "In my whole life I never had so much fun as when Victor lived with us."

Then life was uneventful again—until I began getting all those letters from the IRS. My brother Victor had never paid an income tax.

# The Newlywed and the Hired Man

As SOON AS WE were married we climbed into Pete's old pickup and headed for Aroostook County and his grandfather's old farmhouse. It has been Pete's house since his grandfather died, and now it would be my house, too. I knew I'd feel at home there because I was brought up on a farm in New Brunswick, not far from Perth. I met Pete when he and his friends started coming over to our Saturday-night dances in the Lodge hall. The first time I danced with him I liked his shy smile and the clean outdoors smell of him—like pine, or wind over a field of sweetgrass. Before Mr. Parker's orchestra finished "Let Me Call You Sweetheart," I was hopelessly in love. I'd read about love in the magazines, and I'd had a few crushes on boys at school, but I didn't know it could hit like this.

My folks hoped I'd marry a Canadian boy, but they finally accepted Pete, and they were glad I wouldn't be all that far from home. His family and friends came over for the wedding, and they seemed to get along with my folks. I was so happy sitting in that pickup that I actually felt sorry for all the women and girls who didn't have Pete for a husband. I smiled, thinking of what I'd cook for his breakfast in the morning. I had brought everything I'd need: dishes, tablecloth, and all. I was glad I'd learned to cook from Mama and Gram. Life would be so romantic, me cooking perfect meals for my very own husband in our very own farmhouse.

The moon was shining when we drove in. I thought the place looked as beautiful as any castle in a fairy tale. Pete showed me around the downstairs rooms, and then he took me to our big first-floor bedroom. I guess we were both a little embarrassed, for we giggled and said silly things, but finally we were in bed and kissing and life was sweet. Then I heard rain. "That's funny." I said, "Raining and the moon shining."

"That's not rain," Pete said. "That's Moonie."

"What's a moonie?" I asked.

"He's Gramp's hired man—my hired man now. He's old, and he doesn't like to walk way downstairs and go outside."

I jumped up out of bed. "He's here in the house with us? And he pees out the window? When will he go home?"

"He is home. He has lived here most of his life."

"But he'll move out now that we're here?"

"No. Where would he go? Gram took him in when he was a boy. He adored Gram. This is his home."

"Why didn't you tell me he'd be living here?"

"I guess I didn't think it mattered."

My honeymoon house and my romantic meals were flying out the window. For a moment Pete was a stranger, and I wanted to call Pa and say, "Quick! Come and get me!" But I knew he'd say, "You made your bed. Now lie in it."

My wedding night wasn't as wonderful as I'd dreamed, but it wasn't all that bad. Next morning I got up early and headed for the kitchen, planning to start the wood fire and cook breakfast. I took one look around and said, "Pete, come quick!" There lying on the floor was an old man with his eyes shut. I thought he was dead. Pete came running. By now the old man was sitting up, scratching himself.

"Ella," Pete said, "this is Moonie." We both mumbled something. "Moonie always takes a little nap on the floor while he's waiting for the fire to get going so he can shut the draft," Pete said. "Let's go to the barn, Moonie. We've got a woman to do the cooking now."

I made an omelet with onion and green peppers, toasted some of Mama's homemade bread, fried bacon, opened a jar of wild strawberry jam, dished up fresh peaches and poured cream on them. I made coffee in my new coffeepot. With my dishes and tablecloth, I thought the meal looked perfect when Pete and Moonie finished the barn chores.

"Smells good," Pete said. Moonie sat in silence and didn't eat anything. "Why aren't you eating, Moonie?" Pete asked.

Moonie looked at me. "Pete and me generally have fried eggs and fried potatoes and a pan of biscuits. Don't you worry, Pete, I've got leftovers from yesterday. I'll have it ready in no time."

I hoped that Pete would tell him, "Ella's in charge of meals now," but he picked at my breakfast, and then ate what Moonie had prepared. When Moonie went to the pantry for more biscuits, Pete whispered, "I don't want to hurt his feelings." My feelings were pretty shattered, but I said nothing.

Moonie said, "Tomorrow don't bother with them fancy dishes and tablecloth. Old Missus' dishes are right in the cupboard. I'll show you where." We ate in silence. I tried to eat, but couldn't manage much. Then Moonie said, "I knew you were coming so I saved up my dirty clothes. I'll bring them down, this being Monday. I'll fill the boiler for you this time." Since we had no electricity, I had to scrub clothes on a scrub board, wring, rinse, wring again, and hang them on the line. I hated doing Moonie's work clothes and underwear, but at least I knew how. Washing took all morning. Moonie said we'd have leftovers for dinner—potato hash, cold meat, and biscuits. I was too tired to eat.

When we went to our bedroom that night I had my first chance to talk to Pete alone. "Moonie's a hired man? I asked.

"Yes, but he's more like one of the family. His parents died when he was little, and Gram raised him. Then when he was twenty he met a wonderful girl, Alice. They married and a year later she died having a baby. The baby died, too. Gram

persuaded him to come back here. He's had girlfriends sometimes—women really like him—but he never found anyone he
wanted to marry. He adored Alice."

"That's sad. And you want me to take orders from him? I'm
the hired man's hired girl?"

"Don't be like that, Ella. You don't want to hurt an old man's
feelings, do you?"

When he smiled at me like that, what could I do?

Next day I went out and walked around the place. Beyond
the barn there were three little cabins, which I took to be hired
men's houses. The windows were shuttered, but the camps
looked to be in good condition. That night I said to Pete,
"Couldn't we fix one up for Moonie? Then he wouldn't have to
pee out the window."

Pete said, "He has slept in that room for most of his life. How
can you be so heartless?"

I decided to try hard to get along, but the possibility of moving back to New Brunswick was always there in my mind. In my
first week when I gave the house a good cleaning, I noticed that
the living room wallpaper was dingy and faded from years of
wear and weather. At supper I said to Pete, "I think I'll spend
some of the wedding present money on some inexpensive wallpaper for the living room. I can do the papering myself, so it
won't cost much."

Moonie said, "No you can't. Old Missus loved that paper. I put
it on for her twenty or thirty years ago. It's still plenty good."

I thought of going to college in Fredericton and learning to
be a teacher. That's what my parents had wanted me to do. But I
loved Pete so much I had to keep trying to make the place feel
like my home. Next day I put my little rocking chair beside the
lamp table in the living room. I took the chair that was there up
to the spare bedroom. Next day the old chair was back in its
place. I finally found my chair in the shed chamber with a

lifetime of discarded stuff. That night Moonie said, "Old Missus' chair belongs right here." I knew there was no use to appeal to Pete for support. I kept going to the telephone to call home, but I put off doing it.

Every evening the three of us sat in the living room, listening to the battery radio and reading the paper. There was only one Aladdin lamp, and since Pete and Moonie sat on either side of the table I had to sit too far away to read. I could knit, though. I was making a warm sweater for Pete. Pete and Moonie talked about farm and local doings, so I couldn't join in on the conversations. I tried to be glad that Pete was kind to an old man, but I couldn't be happy here. Yet back home there was a stigma against divorced women. My parents would be shamed.

Then one day I took a closer look at one of the cabins. I said nothing to Pete, but next time I drove into town for groceries I bought paint and paper and some cloth for curtains. I chose the cabin far from the house, and hoped Pete and Moonie wouldn't notice what I was doing until I finished my project. Every day I did all the necessary work in the house, but I was young and strong, and I could plan at least a couple of hours in the afternoon for working on my cabin. From home I had brought a braided rug, a couch spread, books, pictures, pillows, and bedding. I had my rocking chair and I found an old couch in the attic. Quickly the cabin became my home. There was even a little woodstove, so I could make a cup of tea, rock, and read for a while. I closed the window shutters when I left, so I went undetected for several weeks. Then one night Moonie said, "Pete, someone's been snooping around one of the cabins. The grass is all bent down around the door."

Before Pete could answer, I said, "I'm storing my stuff in there, Pete. I go in once in a while, just to be with my own things."

Pete gave me a strange look. "I've come to the house a couple of times and you weren't around."

That night Moonie said to Pete, "Soon as you have a son I'll bring him up same as I did you. I'll teach him to hunt and fish and fight and—" Right then I decided I'd be in no hurry to have a baby, even though Pete and I both wanted kids.

A few days later there was a knock on my cabin door. I opened the door to Pete, who looked around, and said, "Why did you do all this?"

"I just needed a little space that's mine," I said. "I don't feel at home in Moonie's and your house."

"I'm sorry, Ella. I'll try to find a chance to talk to Moonie. I know he'll like you once he gets to know you. Maybe you could paint and paper our bedroom," he said.

"And cover up your grandmother's paper?" I asked. "For now, I'll try to live with things as they are."

If this were a novel, I'd find a way to poison Moonie, I thought. Then I hated myself for being so mean-minded. But more and more I faced the fact of leaving Pete.

One day there was a happy break in my schedule. A local boy who had been hired to help with the haying had gotten the measles, so Pete asked if I'd mind driving the horse so they could get the hay in before the predicted rain. I was delighted at the idea of being outdoors and near Pete all day. My work was caught up at the house, and I'd driven horses at home. But old Star was not happy with me, so he jumped ahead once when I pulled back on the reins, causing Moonie to lose his balance and fall down. He glared at me and stormed over to Pete, saying, "The geehossley hayfield ain't no place for a geehossley woman. Either she goes to the house, or I go."

I held my breath. Pete said, "I'm sorry, Ella. Do you mind? I think Moonie and I can finish up now. Thanks a lot."

I knew when I was licked. If only I didn't love Pete so much; if only my folks would accept my divorce. Then before I told

Pete that I had decided to leave, that old trickster, Fate, got a finger in the pie.

Moonie went somewhere the next Saturday night, and didn't return until late Sunday night. On Monday morning he said, "Pete, I have to tell you something, and I hate to because I know how much you depend on me. But I'll come back and visit often, don't you worry. And you can call me anytime. But I have to leave."

Pete said, "Why? Where are you going?"

"I met this lady who needs a man to run the farm, and to tell the truth, I think she kinda likes me."

"Who is she?" Pete asked.

"She's new around here. Bought the old Adams place on Hill Road. Name's Nancy Grover. She has fixed the house all up. She must have money."

I held my breath and waited for Pete to urge him to stay. But he said, "This is quite a surprise, Moonie, but I've heard of her and I think she's a nice lady. If that's what you want, I'm for it. When will you go?"

"If you don't mind, I thought I'd go tonight." Then he turned to me. "Since this is washday, I'll leave you my dirty clothes. I'll come by Tuesday night to pick them up. You've got the hang of making biscuits now. I guess Pete will be all right."

I managed to say, "I wish you well, Moonie."

That night I couldn't sleep. I redid every room in the house— in my head—and filled several rooms with kids.

Maybe when Pete is a grandfather I will tell him that I happened to meet Mrs. Grover at a Farm Bureau meeting. When she mentioned that she needed a man to run the place, I just happened to mention the wonderful Mr. Moon who worked for my husband, and who might like to manage a farm.

# The Week that Had Two Tuesdays

HERE'S WHAT HAPPENED. My sister Avis and I had planned to start on Monday and spend the entire week doing something we'd put off for years—making family albums for the grandkids. Then it turned out that Avis had a Monday meeting, so she couldn't come up until Tuesday. When her meeting was canceled she left a message on my phone: "I'm coming Monday after all. Have the coffee ready." But my machine is erratic, so I didn't hear the message.

When I saw her drive in I thought, My lord, it's Tuesday! I lost Monday! How can I be so absentminded? Still, it had rained all weekend, and I'd had a stack of mysteries from the library. I fell asleep sometimes when I was reading. I guess I could have lost Monday. I didn't admit that to Avis, though. After breakfast we hurried to our camp by the little pond out back and spread our project on the big porch table. We left my house before the paper came, and since we have neither radio nor TV at the camp, I still thought it was Tuesday.

After we worked a few hours, Avis said she was tired from her long ride, and she needed a little nap. Then I remembered I'd had an appointment to have my hair done on Monday afternoon. I called Cordelia, but I knew she'd be out in her flower garden on such a beautiful morning, so I left a message. "I'm sorry I missed my appointment Monday. My hair is a mess and so is my memory." Later Cordelia said she listened to the message and thought, "It's Tuesday? I thought it was Monday!" But on Sunday night she'd taken a new medication for her nerves. The doctor said it might make her sleep more. But to sleep all night Sunday, all day Monday, and then Monday night? Must be powerful stuff. No wonder I was so hungry this morning, she thought. She decided to make apple crisp and put ice cream on it. After all, she'd lost a lot of calories during the long sleep.

Cordelia is retired, but she still does haircuts for her friends. She looked at her calendar to see what she might have missed on Monday. Her cousin Wimpy Seavey planned to come over Monday night and lay new linoleum in her bathroom. And she had locked him out. She tore Monday off her day-by-day calendar and then left a message on Wimpy's phone. "Sorry I slept last night and locked you out. Combination of pills and old age, I guess."

When Wimpy came back from the store and heard the message, he said, "So this is Tuesday? What happened to Monday?" He and Ross had planned to go up to Harold Brook and catch some trout Monday. He'd been worried about his memory lately. He knew Ross was out getting his mail, but he called and left a message. "I can't explain it, but I lost Monday. Sorry."

"But I thought this was Monday," Ross said when he heard the message. He looked for the paper, but his wife had wandered off with it. She kept telling him his mind was going. Drat it, he'd wanted to see his grandson play in a Little League game on Tuesday morning. Then he remembered he'd promised to take Uncle Clarence up to the Lodge hall Monday night to play bingo. He must have been disappointed. He called the Shady Maples retirement home and asked Agnes to give his apology to Clarence. Clarence was too deaf to talk on the phone. After she gave the message to Clarence, Agnes remembered she'd planned to have supper with her grandmother on Monday night. Poor Gram. Agnes called to apologize.

Her grandmother said, "Honey, are you sure this is Tuesday? I thought it was Monday. I went to church yesterday. I think. Wait until I look at the paper. Yes—the paper says this is

Monday. See you tonight." Agnes wondered if she should call Ross, but then she got busy and forgot about it.

While we were eating supper that night, I said to Avis, "See? We didn't need to work Monday after all. Look at how much we accomplished today."

"Jenny, this is Monday," she said. "Didn't you get my message?"

"You mean we've got another Tuesday coming?" I asked.

I called Cordelia. She'd spent the day in the flower garden, so she still thought it was Tuesday. She had decided she'd better not take any more of those nerve pills. She called Wimpy and he called Ross.

"It's still Tuesday tomorrow?" Ross asked. "I can still see Billy in the Little League game."

Later we all agreed that we took great pleasure in that second Tuesday. It isn't often you have a chance to live the same day twice.

# Tommy Twittering

Dora grew up in a village by the sea. Because she was fair of face, little boys, then older boys, and still later grown men gazed at her and made suggestions: "Want to go out and smash pumpkins?" "Want to go steady?" "How about dinner?" At each question Dora lowered her eyes, blushed, and ran away.

She wanted a boyfriend, though. There was a summer boy she'd seen tooling through town in his Stutz Bearcat. Because he was tall, tanned, and handsome, she chose him for her model when she created an imaginary lover. She decided that he would graduate from Dartmouth and become an archaeologist. On the day when she rocked in her hammock and tried to think up his name, the birds were loudly conversing. She named him Tommy Twittering. She told nobody his name or that they talked for hours every day, or that she went to sleep every night with his arms around her. Decades passed and suitors tried and failed. Dora tried to fall in love with a couple of them, but compared to Tommy they came up lacking. After college Dora came back to Bar Harbor and worked in a bookstore. Later, with a legacy from her grandparents, she bought the store and renamed it "Twittering Bird."

Often in summer a cruise ship steamed into the harbor and allowed its passengers to go ashore. On one such day a passenger wandered into the bookstore and smiled at Dora. She smiled back. Now sixty-four, she had lost her shyness to a point where she could converse with male customers without blushing. This man, like Dora, was tall, tanned, and blessed with a head of silvery white hair. He asked if she knew anyone who could show him around the island. She said she would, as she put the CLOSED sign on the door.

They drove to the top of Cadillac Mountain where he admired the view. They ate lobsters at a picnic table near the shore, they sat for an hour on a bench at Thuya Gardens, and finally they walked along Sand Beach, talking all the while.

"I feel I have known you for fifty years," he said.

"Yes. You seem like an old friend," she said.

When he told her his names she asked him to spell them. When she heard the z, s, and q, she laughed. "I can neither say them nor spell them," she said.

He laughed. "I couldn't either until I was a big kid," he said. "My English-speaking friends call me Tom because those letters appear in my first name."

Dora glanced at him, startled. Oh, well, she thought, Tom's a common name.

They climbed a high ledge so they could continue up the beach. He jumped ahead and reached back for her hand. Soon they would head back since he had to be on board the cruise ship in a couple of hours. Silly old fate, Dora thought. I've never felt this close to a man, yet I'll never see him again.

Then he turned and said something to her. She gasped, and lost her balance. He reached for her, but she fell back a few feet onto the rocks. She lay very still. He bent down beside her, sure that she was dead. A man walking nearby called the county hospital on his cell phone. Soon Dora was on a stretcher. Tom insisted on riding in the ambulance on the short ride to the hospital. He followed the stretcher into the emergency room where an elderly doctor examined her.

"What happened?" he asked Tom.

"She lost her balance and fell on the rocks."

"Hard to believe," Dr. Morrow said. "I've known Dora all her life. She's strong and healthy, and she's climbed over those rocks since she could walk. She wouldn't fall. Did you push her?"

"Oh, no!"

"Of course not. Sorry. Did you say something that upset her? She's very sensitive."

"No. We were laughing about my hard-to-pronounce names."

At that moment Dora opened her eyes, saying "What? Where? My head hurts." The doctor told her she had had a bad fall.

Then she saw Tom. She smiled at him. "Oh, now I under-stand. I'm dreaming. Don't look so worried. You're not real, you see. I made you up when I was thirteen. When I wake up we'll be together like always, Tommy Twittering."

The man with the cell phone had followed the ambulance to the hospital. He asked Tom if he were with the cruise ship. "You'd better get to the pier," he said. "I'll be glad to give you a ride."

"Thank you," Tom said.

"You go along," the doctor said. "Her vital signs are good. She's a little mixed up now, but she'll be fine."

"The last thing I said to her was that my last name translates to 'twittering bird.' That's why I went into her store," Tom said.

The man who offered the ride turned to see if Tom was fol-lowing him.

"I have to stay here," Tom said. "I don't know why, but I know I have to be here when she wakes up."

# About the Author

GLENNA JOHNSON SMITH was born in 1920 in Ashville, Maine, in coastal Hancock County. She earned a bachelor's degree in home economics from the University of Maine in 1941. That same year she got married and moved to a farm in Easton, Maine, where she and her husband raised three sons. She taught English and home economics at schools in Easton, Fort Fairfield, and Presque Isle, and was heavily involved in high school and community theater productions. Presque Isle is now her home.

Her writing has been published in *Echoes* and *Yankee* magazines, and in anthologies, including *Maine Speaks: An Anthology of Maine Writers*. She has also written a number of award-winning plays.

She has received numerous other honors as well, including being named Presque Isle's Citizen of the Year, receiving an honorary doctorate from the University of Maine– Presque Isle, and being nominated for the Exemplary Older Person Award by the state of Maine.

*Glenna's high school graduation photo*